Three Husbands

and a

Thousand Boyfriends

By Patricia L. Brooks

For more information: Brooks Goldmann Publishing, LLC
www.brooksgoldmannpublishing.com
Editing by Kitty Kessler
Interior design by Ann N. Videan, Book Shepherd
1. Memoir. 2. Domestic Violence. 3. Love Addiction. 4. Post-Traumatic Stress
Three Husbands and a Thousand Boyfriends / Patricia L. Brooks
ISBN 13: 978-0-9817881-8-0   ISBN 10: 0-9817881-8-1(Paperback)
Also available in E-book
First Brooks Goldmann Publishing Company, LLC trade paperback edition
January 2016

Also by Patricia L. Brooks
A Memoir *Gifts of Sisterhood – journey from grief to gratitude*

DEDICATION

This book is dedicated to my husband Earl for his endless support of me, my ideas, and my pursuit of the truth in my writing. His willingness to allow me to be myself with this work is a testament to who he is as a person. It is with all my heart I thank him.

ACKNOWLEDGEMENTS

It is with much gratitude that I acknowledge my critique group members who guided me over the past several years. They have spent countless hours helping me own my truth and tell my story. If not for their support and encouragement, this book may never have come to fruition. I could still be silent to the world. I especially thank Kitty, Doray and Pricilla for their courage and kindness.

I also acknowledge the therapists I encountered on my recovery journey, both in group and individual therapy. They generously helped me deal with my post-traumatic stress from trauma and domestic violence, and with my love addiction. It is with their guidance that I came to a place of peace and understanding about who I am and how I am able to help others.

Last of all, I am acknowledging here my friends in recovery who have never left me. They have supported me again and again when I desperately needed their friendship and love. To all of them, I say thank you from the bottom of my heart.

TABLE OF CONTENTS

SHARING MY STORY

Three Husbands and a Thousand Boyfriends explores my many years in love addiction, my domestic violence and trauma experiences, and my post-traumatic stress condition. I use my anger at all of it as a force for good, while sharing my recovery journey.

This is my story of personal betrayal, renewal, and the lessons I learned from my abuser and others I allowed into my heart. I share here openly.

This is the path I took and what helped me find healing from love addiction; a disease that almost killed me just like any other drug could do if abused long enough. It was my best kept secret. The post-traumatic stress I endured altered my insecurities, depression and fear.

My words speak to the secrets I kept and what led to my spiritual transformation. From my personal life that held me captive, to a violent act that brought me closer to God, my story shows how I chose to face my demons and my fears.

Like the bear coming out of hibernation in the spring to walk the beaches in Northern Michigan, I was groggy at times; slow, hungry and unsure. The anxiety I faced head-on with these secrets of love addiction and domestic violence was an opportunity for growth, acceptance and forgiveness rather than an element of fear.

"Why didn't you just leave?" you ask. And better yet, why did I, as a single, educated, professional woman with no children, not walk away? Or why did I stay even after he lied and hit me over and over again a fourth or a fifth time?

God did not abandon me when I faced death's door. Like the great ships on Lake Michigan weathering storms, I found the courage to forge ahead with the knowledge of my secrets as my lifeline.

This book is a full-bore foray into what it was like to be captive emotionally, even before the physical violence began to threaten my life. My other, hidden life was contrary to my professional and social life.

Anyone touched by this story will benefit by understanding more clearly the intricacies of love addiction and how it relates to domestic violence. I hold dear the euphoria that came with finishing this book. Meditation inspired insights from my gratitude journal. I wrote relentlessly in that vein.

The purpose of this memoir was to clearly see things as they were and show that to others. I fueled this book with anger while gratefully taking the road to the other side of post-traumatic recovery. I processed my thoughts in therapy to keep from going back to that dark place of depression that comes with abuse and trauma.

I am a recovering love addict with post-traumatic stress on my shoulders. What I did to myself in those years of love addiction are choices I made. How I survived abuse will hopefully motivate others to talk openly on the topic. *Three Husbands and a Thousand Boyfriends* looks at these important and complex issues knowing there are no easy answers.

The book came together by my asking, "What would I like to show about my chaotic life that is hopeful?" I wrote with fierce abandon and raw emotions, like the gull crying in the night for comfort. This is my truth as I know it.

This book is about restoring body, heart and soul as well as mind and spirit. There is no score sheet, no right or wrong, no stopwatch for the sailboat race of life when healing from trauma is involved.

Here is my story.

I Should Have Gone to Woodstock

Getting married is easy. Staying married is more difficult.
Staying happily married for a lifetime should rank
among the fine arts.

Roberta Flack

Fair Time

I should have gone to Woodstock in the summer of '69. My college roommate Sherry was going—she seemed to go everywhere in her yellow convertible. I had my chance when she called for the last time.

"You'll be sorry," she said. "You'll miss all the fun."

Instead I strolled into the County Fair with my sister and two of her friends. Kathy had been working in another state all summer. She included me with her friends and their fun so we could catch up. We conquered fast rides and ate too much cotton candy. Feeling carefree, our sights were set on fun and not much else.

On the way home, as the country road wound around the farm land, my thoughts would wind around the details of my upcoming wedding. My mind raced through the huge plans. Anxiety suddenly set-in and I started hyperventilating.

1

"What is wrong with you?" my sister asked. Not being able to answer her, I squeezed her hand and gasped for air. I was weak as my chest tightened.

Kathy's old maroon Rambler sped beside cornfields on the outskirts of town to the small neighborhood hospital on a hill just above Lake Huron. The red emergency room sign beckoned in the dark as my heart palpitations increased. Before I realized what was happening, the emergency room doctor dispensed an uninvited injection into my arm and a warm feeling instantly came over me.

Although groggy, I heard my mother's apprehensive voice in the next room. Summoned by phone to come immediately, she appeared to fear my possible change of heart for the big day. The wedding seemed more important to her as it got closer—more so to her than to me.

"Why is she so stressed and filled with anxiety?" the doctor asked.

My mother's matter-of-fact response, "I don't know; she's getting married Saturday."

COLLEGE LIFE

He was a senior on the third floor in the experimental coed dorm where I lived at Northern Michigan University. I was on the first floor with the freshman girls. My parents had given permission in writing for me to live there. I had good grades and was a leader in high school so I qualified for this venture.

My roommate, Donna, was a high school friend. We had been cheerleaders and flute players together and knew each other pretty well. Her high school boyfriend, TJ, was in Vietnam and she wrote to him daily. She studied hard for a nursing degree, planning to go home to our little town and make a life with him. I had no such plans. I was in the business program looking for a new adventure.

I was very excited about my new-found freedom on campus. Although there were strict rules in this dormitory arrangement—the only one like it on campus—it did not take long before the doctor's son noticed me and began a conversation one evening in the TV lounge. He was charming and I was flattered to have impressed a senior.

"What are you studying?" he asked quietly, as he sat down next to me.

"Business—I want to have my own business someday," I chirped.

"That's quite ambitious," he smiled.

Alan was from a professional family and had once belonged to the Gross Pointe Yacht Club in Detroit. Planning to advance to a graduate degree in theology at the Presbyterian seminary in Dubuque, Iowa the next year, he looked to me to join him. He opened the perfect door for my exit out of my small town in the far reaches of the upper peninsula of Michigan. I felt my life would be a dead end if I stayed there. I was sure I would die of sadness, even amongst all the natural beauty of the place. I could not see myself getting out of there on my own without marrying someone who could take me to a bigger place and more adventure. My addiction to an image of love I conjured up was manifesting itself.

The Decision

I should have gone to Woodstock in the summer of '69 to wear red and yellow field flowers in my hair. I should have crowned myself with a head ring that cascaded brightly colored ribbons down my back. Instead, I would be adorned in an eight-foot hand-made organza veil trimmed with tiny white ribbon roses on top of a white satin pillbox hat.

I easily said yes to the doctor's youngest son just six months into the relationship, although he had alluded to the idea from our first meeting. My tall, lean, blonde, blue-eyed boy from Gross Pointe Farms with plans to become a Presbyterian minister was my chance to rise up and out of the lower rung of society— or so I thought.

He recruited me to Campus Crusade for Christ and I went willingly. Faith, Growth and Fruitfulness was the mantra for their values and I bought it all. I was hungry to be a part of something new. It was as if he was my destiny. By going with him to graduate school, changing my life completely from his promise of a bigger life, a more ardent adventure, I made my bed early.

I should have gone to Woodstock, smoked a little Mary Jane, listened to great music, played in the mud and made love in the rain. A totally different story of passion and fun and who I really was would have been written. A marriage at nineteen years old would be the first of many hasty decisions to come out of my desperation to change things I did not like about my life— a life that was already beginning to unravel.

The summer of '69 was not the summer of love for me. Saying yes to the wrong guy at the wrong time because he was the first one to ask me was insane. I was running away from home with no guidance and no direction. I was caught up in my early years of love addiction and dependency on men and had no idea it existed.

We bonded loosely in Campus Crusade for Christ, but I never really felt like I fit in with the group. As the months went on, I spent more time with his friends planning our ministry than with my friends enjoying campus life near Lake Superior. I lived on the surface of much of their conversations. How could I have thought that would be enough for me?

"Are you bored, my dear?" he often asked, as he drew on his pipe.

I should have gone to Woodstock to follow my wild streak, let it all hang out and celebrate peace and love and to feel groovy in that muddy field. Instead, I chose to wrap myself in my fear of loneliness. I could not get enough attention. I was starved for it.

My need for attention was an obsession and I searched endlessly for it. I settled with him. I did not love him. I did not look beyond what was in front of me to see the breadth and depth of the consequences of my decision. The shame and the guilt I felt later were nowhere on the horizon that summer of '69. I stuffed those secrets away.

5

Patricia L. Brooks

THE MOON WALK

I spent my last teenage summer at home with my mother and youngest sister. We huddled in front of our black and white TV in the corner of the living room to watch the first man to walk on the moon. I was numbed by my life changing so quickly and not excited by the historic moon walk. I could not comprehend the importance of either event. We discussed both very little.

I subconsciously knew I was running away but I could not speak those words. There were no ears to listen to me anyway. My mother was never one to sit and talk with me, and I never felt able to confide in her. She did not analyze situations and she made very few decisions. My sister was five years younger and only interested in her friends. I was alone. I never thought to contact my fiancé at school. We spoke on the phone only a few times that summer.

The elegant china and crystal gifts from our registry at J.L. Hudson's in Detroit poured in to my parents' living room like a tidal wave. My mother was in awe and lived vicariously through my wedding. She had never had much, and seemed to long for the finer things in life. She had not seen such gifts before and held each one carefully, as if it were more precious than life itself.

"They look so expensive," she said, with hands trembling. "These gifts are beautiful. Will you take them all with you?" she asked timidly.

"Well, why not? What else would I do with them?" She did not deserve my flippant comment, but I could not help myself. Was she hoping I would leave a few behind for her?

I should have gone to Woodstock to love freely and receive love. By challenging my parents and making my own life decisions I might as well have been living on the moon. I was disconnected from everyone and had very few people in my life that summer.

My last summer at home was not spent with my high school friends on the shores of Lake Michigan at the Sand Dunes, as we had just a year earlier. I was totally focused on my wedding. Some of my friends lived elsewhere and attended summer school or worked in another town. Even my maid-of-honor was not consulted on decisions; I hardly even saw her that summer.

Things had really changed in that first year after graduation. None of my friends understood my decision to get married. Why would they?

In their eyes Alan and I were an odd couple and we were too young. And we were obsessed with what we wanted.

THE FAMILY

My life as a teenager was very different than Alan's. We were from two vastly different parts of Michigan. He knew private yacht clubs in a wealthy Detroit suburb called Gross

Pointe Farms, and an expensive, highly active summer camp in Algonquin Park, Ontario, Canada.

I knew working as a waitress on the night shift at a truck stop during summer breaks from high school and once attending nearby Michigamme church camp in the north woods of the Upper Peninsula.

We grew up worlds apart. My small high school was in a tourist town at the Straits of Mackinac over 400 miles north of the private academy he attended in Detroit. My parents were not part of the social society of our little town. My dad was a loner and worked construction on the Great Lakes, away from home most of the year. My mother was active on occasion at her church, the Methodist Church, but had only a few friends. She bowled on the women's bowling league when my dad allowed it.

Alan's mother served as a docent at the Detroit Institute of Art and lunched with her friends at the Gross Pointe yacht club. His dad was a respected medical professional and director of a small hospital in a Detroit suburb. They knew all the good restaurants, and a lot of the right people. They had connections when they needed them.

My mother saw the marriage as an opportunity. My dad saw it as a mistake, but he did not know how to stop it.

"Are you sure you want to do this?" he asked me one day.

I was torn somewhere in the middle between taking a chance at a new lifestyle and following my gut that said slow down. I made this decision haphazardly on my own, and was feeling strangled by it. I was unable to change anything because I so desperately wanted my life to be better.

"I do. I'm going through with it," I said with determination.

He knew I was not sure and so did I.

I worked late hours that last summer at the local truck stop, leaving me little time to enjoy hanging out with my friends at Chief's Drive-In. I deprived myself of the things I loved when they were there for the taking.

Instead, I painstakingly sewed small pearls along the back zipper of my satin wedding dress and counted my waitressing tips. I stayed on task.

I led a quiet, simple existence before the big event. While most teenagers I knew experienced the summer of love in '69 with parties, the beach and dating, I followed a wedding plan guide from the June issue of Ladies Home Journal. I stayed the course. I believed happiness would just happen when I completed the list of big wedding dos and don'ts. But this was hardly the case.

Sewing my wedding dress and veil engaged me during those quiet summer evenings as Alan finished college. I listened to the quiet sounds of people going down to the beach to watch the boats in front of our house. I was consumed with our special day being the biggest and the best. I didn't take time to attend his college graduation only 180 miles away.

His parents came by to say hello and meet my parents on their way northwest to Marquette for the ceremony. They drove up from Detroit and were in a hurry. They were not interested in the meal my mother offered them.

9

"This is a big day for Alan. He would like you there," his mother said, as she walked her apricot poodles in our front yard. His dad stayed in their black Lincoln and kept the engine running.

"He's okay. We've discussed it," I commented, and backed away from her.

Alan and I did not see much of each other that summer; in fact, we hardly even talked on the phone and I only wrote him a couple of notes. Our marriage was not wrapped in love or romance; not even sex. We both knew it was a marriage of convenience.

We were on a course of loneliness and intense neediness. Was this a red flag for him, too? Did he ignore the warning signs?

"You're not coming up for graduation weekend?" he asked again the next day.

"No, I'm too busy here. I'm in the middle of so many things," I retorted, as if graduating from college should be taken lightly.

My behavior was not odd to me at the time. I did not realize I was protecting myself from seeing what was truly happening. My focus was pinpointed on the wedding. It never occurred to me I was setting the stage for a life apart from him in our marriage.

THE WEDDING

"Are you still sure about seminary life?" he asked as he handed me a silver cross.

"Of course I am," I answered, as I admired the delicate piece sparkling back at me from the red velvet box.

We gathered for the rehearsal dinner at The Flame restaurant in my hometown of St. Ignace. The pink, perfect prime rib was placed before us. The smell of sweet red wine was at our places and all the wedding party and family members were there. Our time had come.

On the day of the wedding, six fine-looking bridesmaids with fresh smiles and great tans matched six fetching groomsmen. Alan's distinguished older brother as best man joined my dear friend Julie as maid-of-honor, along with a precious flower girl named Polly and my nephew Sean as ring bearer. All the girls dressed for summertime celebrating, attractively attired in lime green, long flowing crepe gowns with satin sashes tied loosely at the back. These young women proudly wore daisy and baby's breath floral head rings adorned by white satin streamers. They entered our day as if in a dream.

The youthful men were striking in white tuxedos with black silk cummerbunds and bow ties. Their black patent leather shoes added just a touch of class. Nothing was left to chance; it was a picture perfect day. They were quite an impressive group chosen carefully to share our memorable day. The selection of the wedding party's attire was more painstaking for me than the time spent contemplating what getting married at nineteen really meant.

It was a beautiful occasion for our quaint town and it seemed that everyone was there. The charming site was matched with a warm, balmy, August day. The picturesque, modernistic church full of colored windows and a sharply-pitched steeple sparkled against Moran Bay up a sweeping hill like a jewel at the Straits of Mackinac. It was my mother's church.

A loving crowd of family and friends admired the wild, handpicked flowers from the shores of Lake Michigan that adorned every aisle gate as they took their places. They unknowingly helped us kick off many falsehoods as we began to live our lie. Neither one of us wanted to admit openly that this lavish wedding, the biggest one this town had seen in a long time, was a sham. It was anything but a fairytale, yet we were trying to make it come true.

Foreshadowed by a sojourn to the emergency room just days earlier, our life together was desperate for breath. None of the finely coiffed guests waiting with anticipation in shiny pews knew what transpired at the hospital that night. The emergency room visit was not mentioned the day of the wedding, but my mother carried a small brown paper bag in her white lace clutch purse. If I was going to hyperventilate again, she was prepared. The rescue bag was not needed even though my self-doubt rose to the surface as my new brother-in-law John began the wedding toast. Alan's brothers honored us, but the couple they toasted were people I did not recognize. Were they really talking about us? I felt guilty for portraying someone I did not want to be.

Later that night I remembered only snippets of the day's activities; the music, but not the vows we wrote, the reception in the church, but not who was there. It was almost as if I had an out-of-body experience.

"Did I really get married?" I joked with a friend, just before leaving the reception.

"I'm afraid you did," she said with a low laugh.

We left early from the old house at Graham's Pointe where the after-reception party was being held. We said our goodbyes quickly. I was not excited about leaving the party and it showed. I felt lonely before we reached the end of the driveway, and even worse as we made our way across the Mackinac Bridge to start our honeymoon. The reality of being alone with him and not being interested in him began to set in.

"Smile," he said "we just got married!"

It would be a long week of camping in his parents' Avian trailer. I was now married to the wrong guy. I knew as I searched my heart that lovely night that things were not what they should be for such a big event, but I did not change a thing. I did not turn around and go home. I walked blindly into the night and the honeymoon and seminary life just as I had walked blindly down the aisle that day. I felt sadness that my dad did not approve of the wedding and that my mother did for all the wrong reasons.

SEMINARY LIFE

Being a Presbyterian seminary student's wife soon became unnerving. I was baptized Catholic and attended that church in my youth. I later attended the Methodist church with my mother during high school. I did not feel at home with my husband's religious philosophy or his church of choice. It felt stifling at best.

13

I began early on, after first moving to Dubuque, to make my own version of my reality, a romantic life I shared with my one friend, Charm, who lived next door. She was the only seminary wife I really got to know. I trusted very few people there. They were so different from me, both in how I felt and what I thought.

By wearing blinders, I moved forward, not knowing it was toward an inevitable divorce.

Our socio-economic, political and religious differences soon collided as we began our life together. We did not know about each other, so we grew apart very quickly. The contrast of who we were was too great.

"Are you sure you want to wear that to work?" he often hinted. "What time will you be back? Can I count on you being home at five o'clock for the Bible Study?" he would insist.

We were ill-equipped to make it work, since I felt confined to a small life when I wanted a big life. He wanted to mold me to his seminary world. I supplied most of our income by dropping out of school to work as a secretary, but I could not commit to his church life. I knew very little about it and cared even less. I frequently avoided the seminary wives' meetings and became known as unfriendly amongst the group.

He had his concentrated studies in graduate school along with additional religious classes, plus a part-time job. I had a full-time job working for a charismatic man at a large chemical company on the other side of the Mississippi. I easily found myself very busy and overly involved in work, an escape from boring seminary life.

My time away from the campus also included outside volunteer activities relating to my boss's run for the Iowa Jaycees State President. This commitment allowed me to avoid my real life even more. By working after office hours as a gofer for his campaign, I enjoyed my independence.

Dishonesty was the norm for much of my life in Iowa. I quickly began to live a secret life in an affair with my boss, defying that I was jeopardizing my job, my marriage, his marriage and many of my relationships at work and in seminary.

"People are talking at the office," he said one night when we were out for a drink. "We need to be careful. I have to keep this quiet. My wife would be devastated."

Two years later, I walked away from my marriage and a tumultuous affair with my boss. This secret life had caused havoc for many people, including me and Jack, his wife and kids, my husband, Alan, and women in the office I had lied to many times. I lost my job, my marriage and respect from family and friends. No one was on my side, not even my friend Charm.

"Why didn't you talk to me if you were so sad or unhappy?" she asked me during our last conversation. "I do not understand how you could live this secret life and not confide in me. We are friends, or I thought we were."

I could not answer her and held in my shame. My good reputation and the only friendship that really mattered to me were gone. I left town in a hurry.

With the majority of our wedding gifts unused, I filled a U-Haul trailer and abruptly returned to college in Michigan. My parents and my sisters came to Iowa to pick me up. Jack took us out for pizza and we had a last goodbye. It was a very awkward moment and unfair all the way around. I was selfish for thinking it could be any other way.

Like my life, the gifts looked displaced stored in my parents' front entry. My mother asked once what was in all those unopened boxes and I could not tell her. I did not remember. I had no idea what I was going to do with them. I had to pack for college again and buy school supplies and books; china and crystal were not needed now, if they ever had been.

WOODSTOCK

I should have gone to Woodstock. I would have been the envy of many, but instead I made the decision to marry young and put myself at odds with most of my friends. Peace and love in church did not translate to peace and love at Woodstock.

I should have gone to Woodstock to feel more passionate about my creative side. Woodstock was the quintessential coming of age party. Instead, I left my teen years at the altar and walked into a marriage with too many responsibilities for me to handle.

Desperately needing Woodstock to let off steam and find my heart and soul, I let my spirit soar only in my dreams of how much fun my friend Sherry and the others must have had without me. I never spoke to her again after my freshman year. She never came to my wedding or answered a letter I sent to her the following summer. I severed all ties with her and never looked back. It was a choice that hurt me deeply.

I turned my back on myself, too, by marrying as a needy teenager. I sold my soul out to selfishness and accepted loneliness. Even when I realized I needed space and time I could not stop myself. The downward spiral that began with the wedding was a snowball going down the mountain for a long time. I knew from the beginning I had made the wrong decision, but I did not know how to change it or how to ask for help. Fear ran my life like a wild animal.

Ironically, I lived in a dormitory the year I went back to school after Iowa, with a girl who had been to Woodstock. She epitomized everything I had left behind. I longed for her free spirit instead of hiding behind the shadow of being a divorced student. I told no one of my status, out of shame and guilt. I envied her sense of being alive everywhere she went. Many of us relished her stories of "that weekend" and encouraged her telling of them. I kept my stories to myself.

I should have gone to Woodstock as part of my spiritual quest, to touch the earth and feel nature. Instead I was the expatriate seminary student's wife with a concept of God I could not explain. I yearned to be void of loneliness and not wander from one empty place to another. There were lessons to be learned about myself—patience, gratitude and forgiveness.

I should have gone to Woodstock and canceled my wedding. To marry the would-be preacher man I did not love was crazy. That marriage taught me one of the most worthwhile lessons in life: love yourself first and those who truly love you will come to you. Free love was yet to be mine.

It was not really me in that beautiful wedding gown of white satin on that sunny day, but an actress dressed up for a role she was doomed to play. Even the draw of Woodstock could not have stopped this freight train. I lived a fantasy for others in my marriage and a make-believe life for myself that lasted many years. I sought to please most people while expecting attention for me. Life could have been very different for me. I should have gone to Woodstock.

DAY OF RECKONING

Even if marriages are made in heaven,
man has to be responsible for the maintenance.
John Graham

MR. RIGHT

"You haven't been out in months. How about going to The Cabin tonight?" my roommate inquired. "Everybody will be there to celebrate the end of finals."
She was ready to punctuate the spring semester of 1971 before graduation on Sunday. I had been playing catch-up all semester due to my early marriage detour.

"I'm jealous you're out of here," I quipped. I had told only a few people about my seminary life, but she knew most of the story. I had studied incessantly that school year and did not date. I was ready to.

"Let's go. I need a night out."

We walked under the "Welcome to The Cabin" sign and into a room full of energized people and loud music. It was Friday night at Central Michigan University.

"Who's the good-looking guy at the microphone?" I asked the bartender.

He grinned. "He works for Schlitz—one of their marketing guys."

Handsome shot a wide grin my way when our eyes met. The crowd erupted as the music got louder and bodies gyrated to the live band.

"Thank God, classes are over," my friend shouted.

"Well, for a few days," I laughed. "I registered for summer school. I'll be moving to an apartment off campus in a week and heading back to class."

"You look just like Mary Tyler Moore," he yelled in my direction.

I turned around to Handsome's mischievous smile and beautiful eyes above his tweed jacket. Unlike others in the room, he had no army fatigues or long hair from days in Vietnam. My friend noticed, too, but he was looking at me. His long lashes framed his azure blue eyes.

"Care to join me?" He pulled another chair up to the bar.

"Sure," I answered coyly.

We talked for hours. Well, we yelled over the band for hours when he wasn't pitching beer. He was all about playing football and baseball in college and into his Sigma Chi fraternity at Arizona State University. He had graduated five years earlier and was new to the world of sales and marketing. He wore a Gant shirt and penny loafers. He loved steak and eggs and the *LA Times*.

"I was transferred from Los Angeles to northern Michigan last year. I am in the process of moving. I like the people here, but that snow..." he laughed.

I could tell he was a smart guy, a good salesman. I was impressed. I had never known anyone like him before. I loved the attention. I was in the danger zone.

"What are you doing next weekend?" he queried.

"Studying. I start summer school next week."

"How about coming to a golf tournament with me in Detroit?"

I laughed at that one. "I don't play golf."

"No, you watch and I golf with professional ball players from Detroit and Chicago. It'll be fun. It's a big charity event. George Plimpton is the host. Do you know who Plimpton is?"

"Of course I do. The author," I added quickly, "the impersonator."

He smiled. "My company sends me to do these kinds of events. That's what I do for a living—drink beer and play golf."

He didn't look like he was kidding. My summer was getting interesting!

I took the Greyhound bus that Friday to Detroit. Not an easy feat from Mt. Pleasant in the central part of the state. Handsome welcomed me with a hug.

"We have lunch plans with a Schlitz distributor down by the river. Then I'll show you around the big city. Do you know Detroit?"

"No, not really. I have been here only a few times for dinner and the art museum."

21

He grinned. He knew I was from a small town four hours north in the Upper Peninsula, at the Straits of Mackinac. I grew up in Michigan, but had few experiences with a lot of the cities—especially Detroit. I liked the idea of being near the river.

The tournament was full of celebrities from the Detroit Lions and the Chicago Bears, including Alex Karras and Dick Butkus. The Chicago Cubs and White Sox, and the Detroit Tigers were represented in full force, too. It was a wild and crazy day with plenty of testosterone to go around. I had never been to anything like that before. It was exciting, and addictive. I was hooked on the chaos and the attention I received from so many men willing to give it.

SCHOOL'S OUT

By the end of summer school I was enrolled at the University of Michigan-Flint, just a few miles from his place in Grand Blanc. Handsome, who had now become Mr. Right, had seduced me all summer with nice dinners and new clothes, and a Big 10 school, when he made this request of me. I had commuted for months to his apartment in Grand Blanc by bus or by catching a ride with friends. It was getting old and his idea made sense at the time

"It's inconvenient to keep doing this," he said. "Why not live with me and make it easy for both of us? I can afford to help you with school."

I moved in with him without hesitation. I was incapable of saying no to him. No marriage proposal, no "I love you, I can't be without you." I thought about it for a day and then made the decision to change what I had planned for the year. I did the paperwork for my third college registration since high school only three years earlier.

I told my parents my news in a quick phone call. "I'm moving to Grand Blanc to live with someone and go to U of M-Flint," I blurted out. "I've met a guy. I'm bringing him home next weekend so you can meet him."

The phone went quiet. I was going to live in sin. In 1971 that was rebellious, yet so typical of me. I had left home at eighteen, before graduation. My mother knew she couldn't stop me. I was drifting out to sea again without a lifejacket. My divorce had been final only six months earlier.

GOING TO THE CHAPEL

The snow billowed all around us as we ran to the door of the little non-denominational chapel on Court Street near the U of M-Flint campus. It was what he wanted. He had no religious affiliation. He was not raised in a church. This was going to be plain and simple. The court house would have worked for him, too.

I was baptized Catholic, but had honored no church after my first marriage and my Presbyterian seminary experience that ended in Iowa. I was fine with all of it. It was just a ceremony.

I don't remember the minister's words or how long it took. My immediate family was there and his mother came from Albuquerque. The couple that stood up for us was a recent acquaintance we met at the little golf course that encircled our apartment complex. We had spent quite a bit of social time with them, and they knew us pretty well. They were the likely choice to witness this union.

"You look lovely, dear," his mother said as we walked into the chapel with a gust of wind. "I hope you two are very happy. My son does not like to be alone."

My parents said nothing. I did not expect a comment from them. They were usually pretty quiet when away from home. My two sisters, still teenagers, had come with their boyfriends for the party, but not for the ceremony. We were an odd bunch.

"The reception should be rolling when we get there," he said. "The guys from Schlitz are taking care of the beer and wine."

Things got crazy quickly at the reception with all the drinking. His co-workers, who often drank a lot, were out of control. The women who rarely drank were intoxicated. But we weren't going on a honeymoon so it didn't matter to us. We let the good times roll.

"Wake up," he nudged me. "I'm taking my mother to breakfast and the airport. She says goodbye."

We were at the Sheraton out in Flushing. With little romance and too much alcohol, life's responsibilities outweighed the attention we gave to each other. We embarked on our marriage as if boarding a ship floundering at sea.

I rolled over with my headache. "Are you coming back to get me before check-out?" I asked.

No answer. I heard the door close. And so this marriage was launched.

RIVERVIEW DRIVE

"The house will be done by spring. My mother's sending money for the sod," he announced, reading her letter. "She says it is a housewarming gift."

"That's pretty nice," I added. "My parents can't do anything like that."

"I'm buying new golf clubs with the money. We can do the sod in the fall. It'll do better then," he continued. "We'll do the back deck now. That is less expensive."

We never discussed major decisions like this one. He told me what we were doing and when we were doing it. Enough said.

I found peace in my diary. I have no say, no power. I feel lost and helpless.

He picked the plans for the house, found the builder and chose the lot. He led the conversations at the builder meetings. He earned the money and he spent it. He qualified for the mortgage without me. I did not question a thing. I went along to City Bank in Grand Blanc to watch him sign the papers. I was on the beach gazing out to the horizon.

I had no idea what we had in the bank or what we spent each month. I never used the checkbook. He gave me a cash allowance every Friday for my personal expenses.

FIESTA BOWL

"We will stay with my dad for a few days. He lives across from the campus in a house he is remodeling," he said, without hesitation.

We were headed to Arizona. Was it for me to meet his dad or for the first Fiesta Bowl with his Alma Mater, Arizona State, playing Florida State?

"Are you sure we can stay there? Does he expect us?"

He didn't answer me. All I knew was his dad rented a house across from campus and was fixing it up for the owner. I started packing.

This was our first trip together outside of Michigan. I had never been west of the Missouri River and was anticipating quite an adventure. I was naïve in my thinking that I would see a lot of Arizona outside of Tempe.

When the plane landed, we were in seventy-eight degree weather, quite different than the forty-two degrees of Michigan. There was an amazing blue sky, and a sense of happiness everywhere. The big game was in two days and excitement was in the air.

"How are you, young lady?" his dad said, with his hand out as we approached the back booth of Frank's Friendly tavern. It was not quite what I thought a father-in-law would do, but what did I know? I had only had one other up to this point.

"I'm great. It is beautiful here. I love the sunshine," I chirped, trying to make small talk. The conversation went immediately to football and I took my place in the corner of the booth to nurse my glass of wine.

I don't remember too much about the game except that Arizona State won, it was a beautiful day and Trini Lopez sang at half-time. We had great seats in about the fourth row in the end zone. The fans were wild most of the game. The half-time show was fun and entertaining. It was nice to be out of the routine of our daily life and on vacation.

"Let's go to Frank's for a drink," his dad suggested as we left the stadium.

It was his Uncle Frank who owned the local newspaper in town, not the tavern down the street that became our spot for the rest of the day. Not what I planned for a victory celebration. I mostly listened, and drank wine I did not like.

I smiled and made some small talk. My life with alcohol had moved to celebrating in a tavern, which was really no different from a bar or supper club, with one of his business associates. I had made my bed and I would sleep in it.

TONSILLECTOMY

I opened my eyes to the sound of his voice in the recovery room.

"I've accepted the promotion in Chicago. This is a huge opportunity and a great city. I looked at houses for us after golf the other day. I found the area where we should live."

My throat hurt. It was time to go home and rest. I had checked myself in to Flint General the day before. The surgery was with a local anesthetic in a dentist-style chair. I was twenty-one and not a child so this would be less risky.

My husband found this doctor at a golf game with a client. They decided I needed this surgery after discussing my allergies and sore throats. I was alone the morning of my surgery with only the flowers my godmother had sent over for me.

"When do we have to be there?" I asked the next day when I could talk.

"I leave next Monday. You can come in a month. I'll bring you a contract next week when I return. This house will sell fast; we need to move on it." He beamed with confidence.

I did not fight him. I never did. I believed I did not have a say. I was powerless over myself, too. I had no tools to help me ask questions or express how I felt. I was an empty shell and had been that way for a long time.

I finished the spring semester and said goodbye to my friends and to the neighbors. I did not remember him saying goodbye to anyone. He was ready to go. My new Irish Setter puppy was barely trained enough to make the trip.

"Does the yard have room for Casey?" I asked one night on the phone.

I didn't ask what color is the living room carpet or how big is the master bedroom I was too young to comprehend what the move really meant. Getting my Irish Setter ready for stud service and registering at the College of DuPage was all I could handle. How many more schools will there be for me before I earn a college degree and can pursue a career? When will it be my turn to matter when a major decision needs to be made?

CHICAGO, CHICAGO

"The house is pink!"

"No, salmon. It's a good house for us and a great area for investment," he said, as we turned down the cul-de-sac. This moment opened four years of loneliness masked by too many parties, exotic sales trips, ski vacations with the neighbors and a lot of secrets. A life we couldn't anticipate.

"Welcome to the neighborhood," my new neighbor beamed. "We have a great group on this street," she added enthusiastically. "You'll love the clubhouse and the block parties."

"Thanks, we are happy to be here."

"Do you play tennis or golf?" she added.

"I play tennis. My husband is a golfer."

Instead of voicing my opinions, I complied. Why did I say that to her?

I'm not happy we moved to the suburbs. I am frustrated that I have changed schools again.

I wanted to live in downtown Chicago in a high-rise condo and attend the prestigious University of Chicago off Michigan Avenue. But like so many times, what I wanted didn't happen. I didn't even make a case for what I wanted; I just rolled along as if I was adrift at sea.

"I bought you a dress for tonight. We're taking the owner of the Arlington race track out to dinner. His wife will be there, too," he tossed out, as he came in carrying an ecru-colored, full length, wool sweater dress.

"We leave in an hour," he yelled from the lower level of the house.

"I have a lot of studying to do tonight," I complained.

There was no answer. I had to be there and I had to look good. That was the way it always went. The clothes I made for myself would never do for this or any occasion, if he had his say. I had to be charming, smiling and ready to listen.

PACK YOUR BAGS

"I'm in a golf tournament in Puerto Rico in a few weeks. We leave at the end of the month," he said with that grin. "Part of the trip is a Pro-Am charity golf tournament. I will be playing in it for the company."

That's how we traveled. No travel agent or discussions. His distributors or the brewery decided when we traveled. Planning a vacation for just the two of us or even a belated honeymoon to some exotic location was never on his radar.

"You can deep-sea fish or hang out by the pool with the other wives while I golf," he continued. "There will be professional athletes there. You'll have a good time."

How does he know what makes me happy? He never asks.

As usual on this kind of trip, we drank too much, stayed up too late and got too much sun. I was violently ill from the deep-sea fishing trip and everyone else followed suit. I begged the fishing guide to take me back to shore but that did not happen for almost two hours. After the boat left the breakwater, I was a buoy on the deck, bobbing and heaving with the motion. I kissed the ground when we hit the beach again and looked for the bar to settle my stomach.

"You always were a lightweight even in a little bit of motion," he commented.

I sat silent at dinner, pretending to eat. The others talked enthusiastically about our day at sea or their day on the golf course.

From the Caribbean coast to Mexico to Hawaii, the trips continued. A charter plane took two hundred of the Schlitz marketing team to Hawaii that January for a company convention. With more drinking, high energy activities and a lot of sun, the islands gave me weeks of fun and exhaustion.

We were wined and dined in style on the Acapulco trip he was given by his best distributer. We stayed at the luxurious Princess Hotel near the ocean. Again, I made no suggestions on what I wanted to do or where I wanted to go. I was obedient in my duties of small talk and smiles.

Be grateful you're at this beautiful hotel, it is all paid for. Remember, we flew first class. Take advantage of this trip, it could all end tomorrow, I wrote in my diary as I lay by the pool sipping yet another Margarita.

LET IT SNOW

"Why can't we go by ourselves to Colorado? Aspen must be a great place for a ski vacation," I fished.

"We already asked them. They've made the reservation. Everything is set. And besides, you like them. It'll be fun."

The week-long trip the year before to Vail with another couple had been a disaster. The arguing about too much drinking and where to eat had gotten out of hand. It was uncomfortable almost every day. We hardly had a day without chaos with people we thought we knew. We were wrong.

Why does he think this time will be different? He wants this couple to go because her husband is a wild ass like he is most of the time.

All I could think about was how many times the guys had pushed the envelope and embarrassed me. *I love snow and skiing. How will I enjoy this trip?* I wrote frantically.

"I'm not skiing today. I'm going to browse in the shops for the morning," I announced at breakfast

The constant scheduling was too much for me. I looked for somebody at one of the outdoor bars to talk to me about trivial things, to let the afternoon hours slip away and be somebody else.

"Beautiful here today isn't it?" a handsome, suntanned face said as he sat down near me.

I smiled and nodded, thinking his accent must be German. He seemed interesting enough for conversation. I had another glass of white wine.

THIS IS MY LIFE

At first it was fun. Block parties with the neighbors, tennis with the ladies at the club and taking the L downtown to Marshall Field's. The guys golfing on Saturday gave me more time to study or tend my garden. And when he traveled to Milwaukee for a Division Meeting each month, I had happy hour with people from my office. Life had worked itself out, or so I thought.

"Where have you been? I have been calling for hours."

"I went out for drinks and dinner with the gang after work."

He changed the subject. "I'll be home late tomorrow night. Don't wait up."

"That's okay," I said, "I have class that night until nine o'clock."

That was what it became: having our own friends and our own lives while not being honest and blaming the other for what we let slip away. We had affairs. We drank apart and we drank together.

LUNCH FOR TWO

"I need to talk to you today. I'm coming to get you for lunch at noon," he barked over the phone.

"This must be big. He never takes me to lunch," I told my friend at the front desk. She knew about my affair in the office and raised an eyebrow. I ignored her.

"They fired me. We're leaving here. Give your notice today," he said before ordering. "We'll go to Arizona and buy in to a business there."

"Are you kidding me? I'm not going to live out there in that heat. Nobody really lives there do they?"

He was getting impatient. His eyes glared at me. He had his plans made and nothing I said would change them. Not even my crying or pleading for him to look for a job in Chicago. It never worked. It would not work now.

"I'm buying into a Mexican restaurant in Tempe with a Sigma Chi brother. You're coming with me. We'll be the managers," he continued. "It'll be fun. It's near the campus and should do well."

My soup arrived. I played with it. My mind wandered; *I can end the affair I am having and leave our house behind. But can I say goodbye to the only part of the country I know? Can I live without the beauty of Lake Michigan?* My thoughts raced as he watched me.

We're not a team, we're not companions. Hell, we're not even lovers anymore. I'm addicted to the chaos of our busy life. Infidelity has become my companion. Will the secrets stop? Will this revive our relationship?

ON THE ROAD AGAIN

He signed all the real estate papers at the bank. It was done in an hour; the check was substantial.

34

"I told you that house in Darien was a good deal," our lawyer commented. "You should be able to buy an even bigger place in Arizona."

I sat motionless one more time on the outside looking in on my life. I had not been on the mortgage because women of child-bearing age did not qualify for loans in the 1970s.

I'm numb, I feel nothing. We're moving to Arizona with a pipe dream restaurant business idea from a fraternity brother's voice on the other end of the phone, I wrote that day. *How is this happening to us?*

I was always under his thumb and ashamed of my situation. I had very little money of my own and was afraid of what might happen to me so far away from home. I was dependent on him financially and addicted to the excitement of a life we were leaving behind.

ARIZONA

The stress of a tornado in the panhandle of Oklahoma alarmed my nervous dog in the back of my new Oldsmobile Starfire.

"Why are we driving with the tornado? It could switch directions!" I asked frantically.

"That rarely happens," he snapped. "Can you make that dog stop whining?"

No more company car or expense account, no more help moving. We were on our own heading to the desert. Due to a teamsters strike, the non-union moving company we used lost our furniture for two weeks. The restaurant investment idea fell through before we even hit New Mexico. They found somebody else. Things were getting scary.

"I'm getting my real estate license to join my old roommate in the business. That's where the money is here," he announced soon after we arrived. "You need to get your license, too. We can work together."

"I don't want to be a real estate agent. I'm going to school. We've already discussed this and you agreed I need to finish my degree."

No response. He was already out the door and on to a golf game for the morning.

By September, I was in real estate school and not at Arizona State University. I was studying a topic that did not interest me so I could work with my husband whom I no longer wanted to be around. I was alone often, struggling to adjust to my new life. I was sad and angry, and not receptive to meeting new people in class or in the office.

THE DECISION

Was it the night he put his fist through the wooden back fence of our townhouse that I made the decision to leave? I tried not to agree to buy the big house on the golf course he insisted we absolutely had to buy. I liked the townhouse he bought us before we moved to Arizona. I was settling in to that neighborhood.

Or was it the day he told me his broker signed us up for Marriage Encounter with the Catholic Church to build our relationship? It surely was a time when too many knew too much about our lives.

"Why do we need to do this? You're not Catholic, and you've never gone to church in all the years I've known you."

"It will make our broker, Larry, happy. The office thinks we are having problems. We need to do this," he said, "and besides, you're Catholic, you should enjoy it."

It was not for us and we both knew it early into the weekend. It was designed for good marriages needing a refresher course. An intense program of commitment and intimacy that we could not handle or relate to at any level was thrust upon us. We flunked Marriage Encounter.

That weekend he made another announcement. "My dad's not going to live in a motel on Apache Blvd. We have four bedrooms. It'll work just fine to have him with us."

How will I deal with his dad around us all the time? How can I get out of here?

I kept asking myself these questions when I took the dog for a walk or had a little quiet time to write in my diary.

"My life won't improve, and he won't change," I told my younger sister over the phone, finally confiding in someone. "He doesn't talk to me, listen or care what I think. It's only about him. I can't live this way anymore."

"You better be really sure before you do anything," she offered. "How will you take care of yourself?"

I hadn't made a major decision since I met him years before. But this was decision time. I rented one of our listings—a small condo. I researched the value of what would be my half of what we had together. I applied for a scholarship so I could continue with night school at Arizona State. I transferred real estate offices to get away from him and our broker, who was trying to control our lives. I asked the neighbor's teenage boys to help me move the next week. I only had one more thing to do.

My hands trembled when I faced his father. "I'm moving out today. I'm not waiting for him to come back to town. He is always controlling me. I need to go."

He just stared at the backyard. His chiseled face was stoic. We hadn't had much of a conversation since he moved in a few months earlier. This was difficult for both of us.

My husband was in Mexico fishing. It was rumored they partied more than they fished. There was a chance they could be in jail. None of that mattered.

"I have to go. I am not happy. He controls everything I do. If he was here he would not let me go," I said with my head down. Sadness came over me, but I did not hesitate.

My father-in-law did not move or say a word.

"How could you do this when I'm out of town?" John said as he came through the door of my new condo. "This is embarrassing to me, and my dad. When are you coming home?"

I stared at him, afraid to speak for fear I would do what he wanted me to do. I had to do this. I had no choice. There was no going back.

"I'm not. This is where I live now."

After he left, I cried all night until my chest ached from the heaving. I felt abandoned. I had loved somebody for a long time and now he was gone.

MOVING ON

He married for the third time the next year. His aunt called to tell me.

"You should go and pick up your beautiful china and silver from the house. They are getting married," she said. "It was yours to begin with. He doesn't want it and neither does she."

"Thanks, I guess I was expecting this. I will go today and say goodbye to my Casey dog, too. He was mine, but I can't take him with me."

"Good luck, Dear. Call me anytime," she offered.

Casey was mysteriously let loose after I was there. A friend of mine who worked with the new wife suspected she did it, since she had her own dog and never cared for Casey. That was a sad day for me. I prayed someone kind found him and loved him.

I cried a lot about that day, alone in a bar with a few glasses of wine. I did not cry for what I lost, but for what we could have had. I let a fantasy life control me. I believed someday we might go back to the beginning and that we would change. I was in my late twenties, two marriages down and still no answers.

THE PHONE CALL

For over forty years I believed he had a student deferment during the Vietnam War. But we never discussed it. I perceived him a bit shallow regarding politics or religion. To me, he was someone lacking in strong convictions about the war. And his political affiliation was not mine.

Not knowing these things was as much my fault as his. I didn't share some of my personal convictions before we got married, either. I melted quickly into his world of client dinners, golf, sales trips and business travel. Early on I lost myself, my opinions and who I was. I went along for the ride.

Three decades after our divorce, I called him about his military status. I had called him before, but it was usually about family business and we kept it brief. But this time I was writing about my post-traumatic stress and I wanted answers on all fronts. Some things just didn't add up. I had to write my truth with him.

"Why were you not drafted after your deferment expired?" I asked, after explaining why I was calling. "I need some answers."

He seemed eager to talk. That was not always the case. He told me things that day I should have known a long time ago. Things about his days at Arizona State University.

"At ASU I signed up for ROTC. It was not required. ASU is not a land grant state college," he explained.

This surprised me. I thought he was there strictly for sports, with hopes of a farm team and the major leagues with his baseball.

"I wanted ROTC and Officer Candidates School, and to go to Vietnam," he added before I could respond.

He spent his senior year summer at Ft. Leonard Wood, Kansas to fulfill requirements for OCS with a goal of Second Lieutenant. Then he went on to Ft. Sill, Oklahoma.

My God, why didn't I know this?

"I thought I had OSC and the Army, but flunked the physical. You know I injured my knee in high school and college. It was always a problem," he concluded.

How ironic, a star athlete who couldn't pass the army's physical. Was this a real inequity in life or a coincidence? Was it God's plan?

This wasn't the husband I had known, who couldn't talk to me about much more than "Don't forget beer" or "My tee time is..." or "We're going out to dinner Friday night." I had spent six years with him in three different states, never asking anything but surface questions until now.

His quest for OCS was over after four years of ROTC, four years of preparing to become an Army officer, four years believing he would serve in Vietnam with his good friend; the one who would die there in a vehicle accident. He was done. His military life ended in one short appointment with the Army recruiter.

More than thirty years after leaving him, tears streamed down my face. My big cry didn't happen when I knew about the other women, or when I left him, or even when the divorce was

final and he remarried a year later. It happened decades down the road. I cried because I was finally getting to know him.

Why did he not tell me forty years ago when we were young? How did he deal with this secret? Did he not tell me because I was anti-war, or because he didn't think I would care?

I was easily influenced by him. With him, I had lost touch with who I was and what I was about. It was no one's fault but my own. I left because of the control, not my imagined love fantasy that didn't happen.

Our life together was a part of my alcoholism and love addiction. I only wanted to see the good times, but dwelled on the bad times too often. I was young, and out of place with him, but alcohol made it bearable. Nothing seemed to make sense.

I did everything in a hurry. I abandoned myself. I had good intentions. Many of our friends said we were made for each other. But the truth is I lost myself in fear. I avoided conflicts and did not speak my mind. It took decades for me to see the emotional abuse in this marriage, both by him, and by me, too.

It was not until that afternoon on the phone that I felt true intimacy with him. The ache of love addiction raised its ugly head. Loneliness settled in. I imagined us hoisting a glass of wine again at The Cabin at Central Michigan with big smiles and a bright future.

LOVE ADDICTED

Love cannot be forced; love cannot be coaxed, and teased.
It comes out of heaven, unasked and unsought.
Pearl Buck

I knew in my heart love addiction was dangerous, possibly deadly. Yet it seemed impossible to quit doing what I was doing. I struggled many times to break free, but it had such a hold on me. I was in love with love.

Love addiction is hard to define. It's a craving, a pursuit for identity and acceptance. I was addicted to the feeling of being in love.

YOUNG LOVE

This obsession goes back as far as high school when I learned the one I thought was my boyfriend was spending time with someone else. He was meeting her after work one night, so I hid in the back seat of his car under a blanket. It was parked in the alley behind the theatre. In our small hometown, it was a quiet place. I patiently waited, only to pop up on them after they were parked at the drive-in ready to order.

43

"What are you doing? Are you crazy?" he yelled.

I did not answer. I had made a scene to get his attention. It was surreal. I embarrassed myself, but could not see the insanity. Yet, I knew it was over as he quickly drove me home.

In my diary, I reflected on my growing up years. My relationship with my parents during high school was often tumultuous.

"Patty likes the reckless boys," my dad said one day to one of his friends. He recognized something about me early on but could not name it.

I left home at eighteen, two months before my high school graduation. I wanted to be with my latest boyfriend whenever I saw fit. I didn't want to explain his long hair, his cigarettes and his fondness for beer. I lived in a boarding house with six other girls who had already finished high school. It was an odd situation and I was often angry about my decision.

As the Varsity cheerleading captain, a good student on the honor roll and a flute player in the band, I hid my insecurities behind my need to be involved and to be noticed at school. I was also determined to fill that hole inside me that was love addiction.

My parents had a graduation party at home for me in the spring of 1968. I attended for about an hour, but left early to be with my friends in a cabin near the beach at Lake Michigan. We had secretly rented it for the night. I couldn't see I was hurting myself or my parents.

"We're just friends," I kept saying. I had no intention of living my life in our small town in the upper peninsula of

Michigan, or marrying anyone from there. I fought hard against it even though I had to have a boyfriend at every turn.

I had not sustained a healthy relationship with anyone as a teenager, and by senior year there had been about a dozen boyfriends. I usually chose a boyfriend for the wrong reasons. I needed to live the fantasy of love. Love addiction took over. I didn't know the difference between honest love and illusions of love.

"My relationship with my parents should have been safe and attentive. But it was not; they were not happy. I longed for attention wherever I could get it," I confessed in my therapy session.

"It was all you knew how to do," my therapist commented. "We're going to change that for you."

FREEDOM CALLS

I had affairs in both my marriages as a young woman in my twenties. I married twice for security and for an illusion of love that I did not understand. I was involved with married men in both marriages. They were willing to leave their wives for me, but I had no desire for them to do so. It was not about genuine love and admiration, not even respect. It was the mere ritual of a relationship with somebody who wanted me, who doted on me.

Like any addict, I was hooked early on but could not see my obsession. The excitement and rhythm of it all kept me stuck in my cycle of bad choices. In those days, it was unconscious.

I finally sought a therapist's help near the end of my second marriage. "I will go even if you won't," I told my husband. "I do not want the marriage to end." I vowed that my road to destruction was over, but that was not true. Eventually I left and filed for divorce again, something I would regret many times. I thought I was tired of affairs, but I wasn't. The marriage ended badly, with me in search of myself and that love euphoria—the exhilaration, the thrill I so desperately needed.

Fight Night

Soon after my second divorce, I carried on a relationship with a younger man I met through my real estate business. He was quite naïve, eight years younger than I, and still living with his parents. They were successful real estate brokers in Tempe. He was being groomed to take over the family business.

I knew he was infatuated with me and I worked that to my advantage. I thought nothing of doing what I wanted to do despite his expectations of me and our relationship. One time I ran off to California on a whim with a local bank vice-president fifteen years older than me, just because the opportunity presented itself. It sounded exciting and I could not resist. My boyfriend and I both knew this person.

"Let's visit an old friend of mine in Sarasota. We'll have fun," I suggested when he wanted to get away. "Then you can go on to Los Angeles to the Ali fight," I said, with no qualms about what my young boyfriend might question. I was obsessed with the thrill of it all. I was needy for attention by a new suitor.

I was unaware this man was juggling me with someone else. Ironically, she was in our industry and unaware of me with him. She was waiting for him in LA and oblivious of our plans. He and I had a blissful three days in the Bay Area, as I fooled myself into a fantasy. His lie collided with me inadvertently meeting her through mutual friends at a Women's Council of Realtors luncheon back in Phoenix the following week.

"I was in California last week, too. I went to the Ali fight at the forum," she told our group over lunch. My adrenaline rushed. I was in emotional overdrive. Was I about to hear the worst?

My selfish needs left me standing ashamed of what I did to myself, and ironically, to her, too. I ended my relationship with the younger boyfriend who'd been left behind at his dad's real estate office, due to my guilt and actions. I was exhausted from the highs and lows. As a love addict, I knew I could move on. I had done that before. But it did not end there for my boyfriend.

He smashed in a glass front door panel of my condo the next night, to vent his anger. He was possibly really committed to me, but to retaliate, I had the maintenance man remove the broken door from my condo and help me take it to his new home that was under construction. I shoved it through a window pane to vent my own anger. It was over for us.

I had been under the influence of love addiction with the banker. We had been together many times. He had used me often and I knew it. And I had used him, too. My need for love and attention was out of whack, but I knew how to repair myself.

47

There would always be somebody else. I didn't recognize a pattern here. I was not done yet.

Keep Moving

In my early thirties, I was determined to show the world my independence. I decided I could have what I wanted despite the consequences. This rebelliousness led me to risky business and to doing things I never thought possible. I associated with men I hardly knew and often feared for my life after I realized where I was and that what I was doing was dangerous.

Once I traveled to Las Vegas to a real estate convention with a strange man the same night I met him at a party. He invited me there for the weekend. I went just because he asked me to go and I felt the need to do something wild. I was in that industry, but had not made plans to attend this conference.

While alone in the hotel room, when he was at the tables, I acknowledged I was living a reckless life. For just a moment, I reflected on my sad life.

"This obsession to be with a man, any man, will kill me someday. If I don't do something about this insanity, I'll be dead." I wrote that on a paper napkin and stuck it in my purse. I believed I could correct my mistakes. I was intelligent, successful. I could do this. I acknowledged the familiarity with others, but this was still not yet the time.

My life was prone to things not being in order, often disruptive: alcohol, abandonment, and obsession. I recognized unhappiness, impatience, frustration and anger happening again and again. Chaos was second nature to me, like an old hat you wore walking on the beach.

A new male friend would quickly become a lover. I didn't know how to have men friends as companions. I had no boundaries and was easily infatuated with anyone of the opposite sex who paid the slightest attention to me. I jumped from one to another, unable most of the time to be faithful. I was sure they weren't faithful. My attitude said, "Why bother?"

PORTFOLIO PLEASE

One time I met a strikingly handsome young man with his grandmother at a motivational seminar. He said he had aspirations to work for a modeling agency in New York. We became instant friends that day and his grandmother encouraged us. Since he did not plan to leave for a few years, my obsession with him grew. I worked hard to keep him in my life by being available around his school and modeling schedule and by living his carefree lifestyle.

Although we had a lot of fun together, I was first his caregiver, his cheerleader and his coach until his big break came with a New York agency. Almost everything I did for him was so I could be with him and feel love in a way that could never really be long term. Although I obsessed about making it more than it was, we would last three years. He needed me, too.

He was fifteen years younger than me and a student with lofty career goals. He eventually went across the country when I was at the peak of a successful new home sales career here in Arizona. He was infatuated with me, but not enough to stay or take me with him. We discussed that idea only briefly. I was always going to be left behind.

"You two are good for each other, you are so happy together," his mother often said. She supported the union from the beginning, but knew it would end.

She turned a blind eye to the futility of the relationship by showering me with attention and gifts. I was trapped immediately. My love addiction now had another level, with his parents and grandmother. They kept me in their lives long after he had left, by inviting me often to their home for dinner. Just as it had always been, I was family, I was in a fantasy.

GOLF ANYONE?

During this time, I started carrying on with a well-known and successful professional golfer I met while volunteering at the Phoenix Open. He easily lured me into a three-year affair, with his charm and persistence. He had to have me and I had to have him.

"Give me your number. I'm calling you tomorrow," he said, when I accidentally walked up to him at the bar at Phoenix Country Club. "I missed the cut and I want to spend the day with you. You are beautiful."

I laughed. But after chatting with him briefly, I gave him my number to see if he would call. I had no idea what I would do if he did. I knew who he was and that he was married. His picture had recently adorned the cover of Sports Illustrated. He was definitely a famous guy and my adrenalin rushed.

He called the next morning. I questioned whether it was really him or one of my friends kidding around with me. That would have been like them. They knew I was easily fooled.

"It is me," he laughed. "Meet me and my brother at a bar in Tempe to watch the Super Bowl game. A good friend of mine plays for Dallas. I want to watch the game and be with you and my brother and his friends."

He caused a bit of a stir when he entered the bar side of the restaurant where my girlfriend and I waited. Things settled down in the room when the game started. Then he proceeded to put the moves on me and not watch much of the game. His brother did not seem bothered by any of this. He must have seen this act before.

That day catapulted me into danger, excessive stress and many lies. I almost lost my job and my mind obsessing over him. I was delusional from the start about what we really had together. It was a fantasy life of flying to tournaments and being wined and dined by him and his golf friends. It was insane thinking on my part to believe I meant more to him than just a fun weekend. There were many nights of longing to be with him. But as a love addict, I had to live in my fantasies and not in reality. I functioned no other way.

We couldn't be a real couple, but that was never on my radar. My life was phony. When I flew to visit him, or when he was here to see me, we concocted a selfish time together. I lied to my friends repeatedly when Mr. Golf came to town on short notice. I dropped everything for him. My life came to a standstill. I could not stop doing any of it. He lied to his friends even when it wasn't necessary.

His wife found a message I sent through the tour mail at Doral Golf Club in Florida, something he had told me not to do. But I was too excited about my new condo and getting a message to him to think straight. I was also young, and reckless, and crazy in love beyond anything I had experienced before.

Unbeknownst to me, Mrs. Golf hired a private investigator who followed me for weeks. He reported back to her that he liked me, but that I was a real threat. With this information, she confronted her husband about the affair and admitted to the investigator.

This was just days after we'd spent his fortieth birthday evening together at my condo, while his wife had a large party waiting for him at their home down the street from me on Camelback Mountain.

Mr. Golf abruptly ended the affair with a call to my office. "I told her you're a crazy fan stalking me. I promised I would call you and put an end to it," he said in a matter-of-fact manner. "It has to end now. I have kids. She is threatening to leave and take them. I can't have any of this."

I couldn't breathe as his words hit me in the face. Those three years meant nothing to him. My begging was pitiful and he made no response. My love addiction had now taken me to my bottom.

I became physically sick immediately from his call. As soon as I hung up the phone I heaved like a tidal wave in the office bathroom. I became even more physically ill with uncontrollable crying as the day went on. People were beginning to notice and stare.

I left the office in a hurry. I sensed the pain washing over me. I headed to my therapist in a frenzied state for an emergency appointment. I was going through withdrawal in her office with trembling hands and hyperventilation. I was no longer able to function properly.

"I feel debilitating pain in my limbs. I am afraid I am self-destructive. I don't watch what I am doing and keep dropping things," I told the campus psychologist. "I feel shame, as if I am worthless. I know I'm depressed. I don't want to go anywhere or do anything"

We talked for awhile then she sent me to the Health Center doctor for a prescription for antidepressants, something I said I would never do, but I was desperate. I prided myself on not doing drugs, but a stiff drink was another story. I still couldn't see that my drug of choice was men and that I was highly addicted. It was a dangerous place to be.

CROSSING THE LINE

I am not sure when I crossed that invisible line and changed the color of my love addiction, but for the next ten years I found I was attracted only to professional African-American men. I was consumed by the exotic myth of the black male. I lost sight of who was the right man for me; it was all about their intriguing culture.

My social life had a narrow focus. My time with friends was minimal. I pushed people out of my life and opened myself up to an intoxicating world. My love addiction transported me to a new level of intrigue. The fix now needed to be greater to get that rush.

The magnetism that pulled me to black men was as strong as the gales of November on Lake Michigan. Society at the time was still not very tolerant of interracial unions, seeing them as merely sexual attractions. Some of that was true for me, but as the love addict, it was about the excitement. Younger black men who liked to date older professional white women were vulnerable. I could get my fix by nurturing, satisfying my hunger.

I lived out of my perceived social circle and could not stop this obsession. It had a stranglehold on me. It was my secret infatuation. My love addiction had me in a more dangerous place. I was out of my element, my comfort zone. I was not interested in a relationship with a white man my own age. I was living a clandestine life. My friends saw me as daring and reckless. I made them uncomfortable.

"I don't understand this need I have to be exclusively with black men," I told my therapist. "What is it that is so intriguing about them?"

"You tell me," she smiled.

I didn't love these young men. They did not love me, even if they thought they did. I often felt shame when talking about my life with my friends. I rarely introduced the young men to them or even told them who I was dating. I began years of secret exploration, packing my life into a closet. Only once did I take a young man in this secret circle to a friend's home, but I soon felt uneasy because he was uncomfortable. We left early, and I was later sorry for that decision.

I held my own for a while, but often became angry and frustrated with our conversations. I was cheating myself out of friendship with several women who had been in my life for a long time. I wasn't honest with them, but I could not help myself either. I kept pretending that my life was okay, when in fact it was far from it. I held a lot of secrets from them about where I went and what I did. I hurt myself more than anyone.

I paid a high price for this later when I really needed them to help me. Several of them were unresponsive after being shut out for so long. They did not want to be around me in the end when one of these young men became my abuser. They feared for their lives and their children's lives, too. With a violent man in my life, they feared his jealousy and rage would lead them to danger. Being associated with me was now impossible.

THE ENEMY

Was it a coincidence that I casually met the Enemy, my abuser for two years, on my way home from the movies one night? I doubt it. We were looking for each other. We needed each other. Love addiction brought us together like the sand and the wind find their way to the shoreline each summer.

Out with a girlfriend one evening, we stopped to dance at The Soho Club in downtown Scottsdale. As we entered, the usual crowd of well-dressed men and women lingered at the bar with their reflections peering back at us in the large mirror outlining the dimly lit lounge.

"I have studying to do early tomorrow morning," I insisted to my friend. "We can't make it a late night. Promise me."

But the lure of the sultry, smooth music was tantalizing. I could tell immediately as we entered the club that it was going to be hard to get away. I made bad choices easily in these situations. Although graduate school was important to me, it lost its luster quickly that night. My love addiction was chronic. It took over quickly when the temptation was there.

As a recovering alcoholic with many years of sobriety, my purpose at this club was different than most. I would not be drinking alcohol. I saw opportunity as many of the men in the club were young black professionals. I was home, a chance to get what I needed and move on. I would not walk out even when the negative consequences crossed my mind. Giving my phone number to a person who might pester me and not be what he pretended to be did not deter me. I could not act against my addiction.

Dressed in khaki shorts and a white oxford shirt tied at the waist, I met the Enemy. I looked quite conservative in this crowd. He was dressed in a dark silk suit and Italian loafers, with a handsome mask and an infectious smile.

The Enemy plucked me out of the crowd quickly and the deceit on both sides began to dance. He smiled and took my hand, pulling me closer to him. No words were exchanged. I let my guard down. There were no warning signs. He didn't alert me that he was controlling or abusive. He didn't tell me manipulation was his game. His dark eyes never left mine as if to hypnotize me. He drugged me with his stare. We danced and watched each other as if we were both stalkers. I felt uneasy at first, but couldn't stop playing our game.

Did he sense I was exclusively dating black men? I had played cat and mouse here before; had he seen me here? He seemed on a mission. I could feel it by the intenseness of his grip. He could not take his eyes off me. By the end of the night, we were out to breakfast just down the street. We talked until four in the morning when the place closed. I gave this man the chase he wanted by being coy, yet offered little about myself as he studied me.

I did not find him particularly my type, with his fancy shoes, exceptional good looks and overdressed suit. He was a little too perfect for me, too pretty. But his professional air of confidence meant he was someone I could spend time with if he asked. I would make it happen. I would fantasize about who he was and what he was about.

We shared graduate degrees and took pride in the educational decisions we had made. He was a research scientist with a lot of responsibility. I was a successful sales and marketing person ready to expand my career. But low self-esteem, insecurities and bouts with depression we both tried to hide were critical red flags in the relationship.

Ironically, our physical health was actually at its peak. Although he was eight years younger than me, we could go out and jog for miles together. We maintained exercise routines as competition more than companionship, only reinforcing the theory that abuse is a game of power not sex, a game of control.

On a trip to the Bay Area of California at Christmas one year, we jogged for an hour on a cold and cloudy day in sleet and rain just to prove we could do it. Looking back, it was definitely a power play that made no sense.

I rebounded from his abuse and took him back time-after-time, mere weeks after vowing it was over. Despite his lies, transgressions and violence, I denied it all and jumped back in. I couldn't slow down. My abandonment issues were healed as soon as he uttered a few kind words or offered flowers with a night out to dinner. I was off and running when that euphoric high kicked in and I felt wanted again.

At this point, my friends were no longer willing to listen to my tirades about him always being late or what he did with other women. They no longer invited me to lunch to have me lie to them about what I was doing with my time. They didn't want to hear why I took him back in to my life when I made excuses for not keeping invitations with them. They did not want to have me justify the bruises and embarrass myself for them.

"How did I get to this point? What has happened to me?" I asked at the initial group meeting. "I am a crazy person. I don't know myself anymore," I said sheepishly.

"You are just beginning to know yourself after a long time being lost. This all needs time. Prayers will help. You need to find forgiveness for yourself first. You need patience with yourself," the group leader offered.

Beginning of the End

Wherever there is danger, there lurks opportunity;
Wherever there is opportunity, there lurks danger.
The two are inseparable.
Earl Nightingale

The Assault

I sensed he was still there. The tenseness in my limbs and the tightness in my chest meant trouble lurked nearby. I could barely hear my breath or feel my heart beat. Was I dying?

An oozing warmth on my neck felt similar to the hot oil treatments I had done to my hair. Reaching up, I touched the throbbing part of my head and realized I was cut open, my blood seeping down my neck. I feared he would finish the job this time. Was this the beginning of the end for me? Was he trying to kill me?

I was sliced vulnerable by something strong enough to put a large gash in the back of my head. My mind slowed to remember in the white fog, as I hovered over the chaos, my place in the safety of shock, when pain stifles and trauma and is accepted.

My reflection frightened me in the full length mirror on the wall. I lay flat against the crumpled, white, hand-woven rug next to my bed, my face red from exhaustion. The rug's loop design pushed imprints on my swollen face. Panic pressed me harder to the floor like a smashed-out, small, defenseless bug. Imprisoned by the awareness of how isolated my world had become, the walls closed in on me. I needed them to embrace me, but they could not. I was truly alone.

I saw his face this time, but just for a moment: that intense glare, those angry dark eyes looking for prey. I heard his teeth gnashing; the fog descended. I must have hit the back of my head on the far corner of my small European antique dresser. There was no other sharp-edged object nearby.

This room was my sanctuary for sleep and reading, but had also been the scene of other painful moments. This was not the first time I truly feared him in this room. Several times he tried to cut off the air in my windpipe, saying it would intensify my sexual arousal, but I would not agree. These walls held stories of his brutal acts of terror. Now they held the key to our final chapter. If only they could talk and help me remember how vicious he had been this time.

THE RAGE

He had entered my apartment abruptly through the patio door I had forgotten to lock after watering the plants. The one time I didn't remember. The repeated trips in and out had distracted me from locking it, even though I always locked it, double-checking it each night.

The impact of his brute force against the door's steel frame startled me as he jumped onto the sunken patio from the wall above. He appeared so quickly I could not anticipate what would happen next. He broke in with great determination to get what he wanted. He raged with arms flying. "You bitch. How dare you ignore me?"

That vicious look in his eyes had a force beyond what even I believed possible. He came at me through the dining area, pushing down chairs. "You have been ignoring me. You did not answer the phone," he insisted. He dragged me through the hallway to my bedroom, where he beat me.

I had seen a lot of his rage before, but that night he was out of control. He broke my crystal vase on the side table in the hall with his right arm, as he grabbed my hair and dragged me down the hall toward my bedroom. *Would he be the death of me? Would we get to a breaking point? Was this that night? I was suffocating with terror. If I denied his escalating rage, would I avoid another fight?*

He was not going to leave until something terrible happened. He was possessed, ugly, intent on hurting me.

"You ungrateful bitch, you can't say no to me."

Spit spewed from his mouth. His face purpled, his jaw set. His once handsome face and charming persona were nowhere to be seen. He was a monster in a silk suit.

I saw fear in his eyes as he rushed at me again. I felt desperation as he pushed his weight around to get to me. Did he finally realize that I was really done? That I had crossed the line? Our years of lies, disappointments, coercion, power and control had built to a crescendo. The force of it was there in that room as I tried to feel my way out, but was caught easily by his strong hand.

He frantically attacked me as if he were a rabid animal. He pushed me hard to the ground and pounced on me. I was unable to respond, but for a few chances to scratch his face. In this rage of high intensity there was no going back. He took control in that small bedroom the only way he knew how; with extreme violence and strength over me, forcing me to the white fog where I could emotionally survive.

THE ENEMY

Frightened to my core, I stayed inside my white-fog of protection that would not let me fully experience all the abuse. This assault was our swan song, the crash of the vessel against the shore. God knew I could not go at it again the way I had before. I was all alone. The fog set in with the first punch.

I slowly opened my eyes and raised my head as my view of the room came back to me. I did not want to alert the Enemy. A tidal wave of questions threatened to carry me away. Was he gone? Was I alone? Would I survive?

An arrogant smirk appeared on his chiseled face, like a distinction in a well-cut stone. There he was, so familiar and dangerous, as if he had a right to hurt me.

I saw his wide feet next to the spots of bright red blood on my favorite white rug. They were planted firmly next to me like a piling holding a dock in place. He often tried to hide his big feet in expensive Italian shoes, but they usually looked out of place, just as they did that night. He tried to hide his broad body in tapered European silk suits, too, but they never quite fit, rising up with his movements.

The Enemy weighed a hundred pounds more than I did. He had been an award-winning weightlifter in high school and college and still maintained some of that strength in his thirties. He was eight years younger. He knew precisely what he was doing when he physically tried to overpower me. He was an obstacle I could not overcome. His advantage wore away at my psyche like an old mooring rope, frayed and stretched to breaking. I prayed this was the last time.

The Enemy was naturally stronger than I was and he worked at it, training at the gym. When it came to brute strength, he won. And he knew it. This time was different though; I was unable to fight back as I had previously. My fear depleted my strength. Did he observe me in the white fog and back off? Or was the severe gash in my head a trophy for him?

He had ignored my phone calls all week, as I tried to confirm our weekend plans. He actually believed that I was the cause of this confrontation because I did not understand his needs. He lied to me again about where he was and what he was doing, as he had done so many times before. Keeping control was his way of handling our relationship. My love addiction controlled me, too, and I could not stop any of it.

His aggressive behavior, though sometimes passive, restrained our relationship. When he threatened me, I usually froze in fear, even if I was angry. We got nowhere because there was no answer for me. If I fought back I suffered even more at his hand. He acted out and raged often, and sometimes I did, too. I couldn't resolve anything because we were in a storm that kept getting worse.

GOD'S GRACE

The Enemy did not anticipate God calming me. Nor could he visualize me finding my way through the white fog to live. He did not expect my escape from him in this storm, since he had won many times before.

The white fog was real. That misty haze hovered over the top of the crime scene. My mind would not go deeper to my truth. My soul was unwilling to chance what it might learn. This was God's grace at work.

I was frozen. It was as if every one of my body's vital organs shut down and death crept toward me like an incoming tide. I didn't flee because being motionless was my only defense, so I played dead. I could not struggle with him. I was in a new and quiet place. I reached deep for my faith. I withdrew into my soul.

Will he let me go? Will the sight of the gash and the blood startle him? Has he reached a boiling point? Will he go where he has never gone before? Will he kill me? Will he realize this assault means big trouble for him? Maybe jail time?

My thoughts cleared when I realized he was in the bathroom. I pulled myself up off my bloody rug and escaped back down the hall. The will to live took over. My chance to cross to the light and die at his hand had never been so real.

Even though I had feared for my life for over a year, and ached for my lost soul to return, I did not bow down this time. I prayed for forgiveness for my part in our chaos. I weathered the storm. I had sought dry land many times before, but this storm took me deeper into the sinkhole of our relationship muck.

ARTWORK

The blood was everywhere. It followed me, staining my pastel sheer robe as I ran. Red spotted the light tan carpet, splashing fear across the back of the white glossy front door in the living room. My bloody handprints were a loud crimson contrast against its whiteness. They were vivid, a child's artistic expression for help. I regressed to that little girl who felt alone many times. Fear of abandonment permeated my space. I recognized it. I knew it well, having lived a life of secrecy and isolation in this violent relationship.

My bruised and bloody hands painted indelible patterns on the door. I braced myself on the frame. "Please, God, help me." I was frantic, forcing my little remaining strength on the dead-bolt and chain that continued to hold me captive.

Struggling to get out from this prison, like the fish that battles from the hook, I fought hard and sprang loose.

He was inches behind me as I lunged out the door to solid ground and some safety in the outside courtyard. I felt his heavy breathing behind me. He would not let me go easily. I had to keep moving. He didn't necessarily want me, but he didn't want anyone else to have me either.

The Enemy had scratches, but no bruises that I could see as he appeared in the corner of my eye. His dark skin against the shallow light of dusk inhibited my view of him. He knew me to fight back, but this night indicated a different kind of struggle, a powerful surge on his part. He was unstoppable.

"Please, God, help me."

I sprinted across the courtyard to the stairwell closest to me. He headed to the parking lot, as if a retreat was all he had left. He may have underestimated me that night, but I did not underestimate myself. Not this time; my adrenalin was running full speed ahead. As I found refuge, he looked back one more time, still showing that vicious face of indignation.

THE RESCUE

Hearing my upstairs neighbor's voice, I ran up several stair steps toward her. My hysterical yells helped her find me.

"Help me. Help me."

This was my chance for a safe haven, a warm feeling of someone caring, even if only for a moment or two.

There were only a few people in the neighborhood on that holiday evening. God led me to the one woman who was willing to help me. I knew her only casually; she waved in the mornings. Had she been waiting for me to ask her for help?

Now, confined to a small space near the stairs, my mobility was minimal. Her second-floor apartment was visible to me. She was willing to help me, with no questions asked. God's grace enabled her instinct and heart. She was not afraid to partake in something that held danger. Her heart was in the right place.

Like the brave storm rescues I knew from growing up on the Great Lakes, she heeded the call. She was a lighthouse in the darkest of night, a beacon of hope.

With her boyfriend and his friends watching the Fiesta Bowl game blaring from their TV, she stood ready by the door. She had heard the noise, the screams. She knew this day would come. She came quickly to me with a soft towel for my head and a kind word to soothe me. With her gesture, the feeling of comfort after a warm summer swim came back to me.

She was not talkative, just needing to be kind in her own silent way. "I've called 911," she said. "He's left—you'll be okay now. The guys upstairs in the other building saw him, too."

"Thank you. Thank you."

She wanted to help; it was her nature. She gave me her weak smile. I thought maybe she had walked in my shoes. Who was that man always around her apartment? He never said hello.

She reached out her hand. It was small and dainty; she wore no rings. "Come inside," she motioned to me.

"No I can't let anyone see me like this."

I began to feel humiliated as I hovered in the stairwell. My shame had surfaced. I could feel it, but I had a friend.

The men in her apartment did not respond to us, as if screaming women and bloody towels were part of the norm. Perhaps he did not want to get involved, or maybe they were desensitized by the inherent violence of football. Or they could have just been mesmerized by the game.

She waited with me and talked a little in a quiet voice, as though she were a member of the "sisterhood" that had survived violence. "He doesn't live there does he?" she asked sheepishly.

"No. He has been coming around for a couple of years, but no more."

She was older than I expected, pretty in a plain sort of way. Her face glowed from the sunset on her cheek. This day she came closer to me by leaning in to listen. She was stronger than she probably appeared to the ones engulfed in football. I could sense it.

Two younger male neighbors on the third level in the next building were watching us. I wondered how long had they been there. I didn't know them, but I guessed they knew me because they had quite a view from the third floor. Peering down at us into the courtyard, one waved slightly. I did not respond. I was almost numb.

Had they seen the Enemy run away? I prayed they were waiting to tell the police about his threat. Did they come to my rescue, too, and record the license plate and get a firm description of him and his car? Was this their chance to have some control over fear and intimidation? Please God, let them be another source to my truth.

It's a miracle that I fled. I barely escaped intact. God gifted that to me. The Enemy had done cruel things before; yelling vulgarities, hitting and slapping me, shoving me, pulling my hair, banging my head on the trunk of the car and shoving me out of the car. Violence with us was not new. I had faced Death's door before, but this time it was too close.

THE HELP

Two male paramedics, two male police officers and a policewoman arrived promptly without much fanfare. They took charge immediately.

"Come inside. We need to take a better look at you in private," the first officer said gently.

They had been called before; once by me and once by the neighbors. This location was in their files. They were not surprised by what they saw when we entered the light of the condo.

They had done this type of rescue many times, and it showed in their actions. They were thorough in their questioning. I sensed they cared, so for a few moments my guilt and shame were at bay. They were kind and professional.

"We need to ask a few more questions," the lead officer continued. "Are you able to help us with this? Will you be testifying if we need you?"

While the paramedics tended me, my exhaustion took over. I let go quietly and slumped into the dining room chair they had pulled forward for me. This release was like the sensation of surfacing rough waters after going deep and then hitting the beach. A calming rush came over my entire body.

"I want to help," I said. "I want to end this."

The female police officer gently held my hand. She was petite in stature and appeared almost timid. I sensed a quiet strength; she had more experience than was obvious for her young age. She asked no questions.

After cleaning my wound, the EMTs wrapped my head carefully with a large towel-like piece of gauze that applied some pressure. They were gentle and efficient.

"Do you know what you hit your head on?" the officer asked.

"No. I remember very little, but maybe the dresser. He came in through the rear patio door off the kitchen. I had left it open by mistake. He jumped down from the raised parking area to the sunken patio." I pointed in that direction.

"Did he sexually assault you?"

"No. I don't think so," I said as I looked away.

"You can get dressed now," the EMT said. "We're taking a trip in the ambulance to the Emergency Room. You should not drive yourself."

This shame-filled night moved forward. I wore dried blood, a gauze head-wrap, scratches and bruises. I had fought back. The signs were evident. At least they were to me.

THE E.R.

The admitting staff at Scottsdale Memorial's Emergency Room had a lot of questions. It was agonizing to do this alone. My neck was tense and my thoughts raced like a heavy wind. My heart pounded as if to burst and my body was stiff with fear. I knew this night was far from over. The ER was busy, yet I did not want to go home.

"The white fog protected me," I told the young woman in front of me at the reception area. She smiled. "The bloody hand prints on my front door show my terror—a record in case I need it. All the air left my lungs with the last hit. God cannot be everywhere, so I left my mark."

There was no response from her. She kept methodically processing paperwork.

"There was no rape evidence taken by the police," I continued. "They only asked me a few questions and checked under my fingernails."

Was I in denial of rape and pushed it deep? Was it too painful to consider or admit?

"I don't believe he came for rape, or that I was raped."

He came to stake his claim because he knew he was losing control of a possession, not a love, but an obsession. He had to have his way. It was all about power, not sex. My thoughts were running wild.

"This time he almost killed me," I blurted out. The clerk didn't look up, but called for the attendant to take me back to the exam area.

As I lay there in that sterile bed, my thoughts were a blur, my heart beat faint and my breath was not in rhythm. It was a shameful place for me. I imagined the nurses feeling sorry for me and asking each other why I did not just leave him. They kept asking me if I needed anything, as if I could possibly know what I needed, when I obviously needed everything. God would bless them for trying. I shuddered to think of what could have been if he had not stopped.

I was bloody, sad, lonely, tired and angry, beaten, bruised and cut open. The main nurse sent in the attending physician to close up the oozing wound. He quickly moved to the opposite side of the bed before I could take a good look at him.

"Hello. I am here to suture your head wound," he said.

"I think it's deep." I tried to make conversation.

He got down to business, cutting, wiping and inspecting. I winced a couple of times before the anesthetic set in.

Was he tired of seeing abused women here? Why did he not order an X-ray or MRI? Was this not serious to him? Was it because I did not have insurance? Was he angry for having to do these senseless stitches that could have been avoided?

His inattentiveness to me personally added to my humiliation and shame. The gash in the back of my head took ten stitches. It was profound and it would take time to heal. So would I, but I would find my comfort elsewhere.

I bore his frustration as he asked me a few nondescript questions. "Does it hurt? Did you pass out? Are you dizzy?" He appeared unfazed by what I had endured and worked quickly.

He stood behind me as if he did not want to be recognized. I could see he was of average build with dark hair and dark skin. Why was he ill-equipped to know what more to say? His life experiences may have prohibited him from comment. Ashamed to be there, I fell into my insecurity and asked for nothing.

I asked myself many questions to occupy my mind as the doctor finished the job. *Why is a gash to my head not worth a small conversation? Am I just another stupid woman in the ER? Does he empathize at all with my heartache? Doesn't he have some sense of responsibility as a medical professional to do more than just sew up my head? Does he not know what to do, beyond sutures? Does he care?*

Does he see this scenario often? Does he see too much abuse? Has he become numb and shut down? Is he getting traumatized, too, from witnessing too much, too often? Does he remember I had been in the emergency room a year earlier, when my head was smashed against the hood of my car?

I chose to forgive him and to look ahead. The reality of the night was more apparent and I had to move on to somewhere, to something else.

I tuned out the sounds of the hospital to help me accept my situation. The humming of the equipment, the patter of nurses, the voices behind curtains became soft white noise. It was the only way I could cope and stay in the moment. It would soon be over. I asked God to show me a sign.

"Do you have a person who will come pick you up?" the nurse asked. I gave her the name and number of a friend. But this was a holiday, and my friend had two young boys home. I was asking a big favor of Diane, but the nurse made the call. Since paramedics had insisted on driving me to the hospital, I would not be released on my own. I needed to ask for help.

This was just the beginning of the end with the Enemy. I knew it in my heart and I was ready to take the next step—from victim and witness, to survivor.

THE SOJOURNER CENTER

Good friends are like shock absorbers.
They help you take the lumps and bumps on the road of life.

Frank Tyger

THE JOURNEY

"I reserved a safe place for you to spend the night," Diane said with her usual take-charge attitude. "I called a women's shelter. They have space for you," she continued before I could comment. "It's the Sojourner Center in downtown Phoenix. About thirty minutes from Scottsdale."

I was not happy about the idea and did not want to go, but I knew I needed shelter from the storm. Who did she think she was, telling me what to do? I was a grown woman. I had a mind of my own. I could make my own decisions and my own mistakes. Yes, many of my past decisions had nearly cost me my life, but I was tired of being told what to do. I was angry, defeated and ashamed. She knew it, too.

How can she even think of making a decision to take me to a strange place? I am mentally and physically weak from the night's trauma. I am tired and humiliated like the fish that doesn't get away and finally succumbs. I want to hide from the world. Maybe I can hide in that place for a day or two and then go home.

"The stay is thirty days," she added quickly, "like we did in recovery."

This was unacceptable to me. The idea felt suffocating. I had almost drowned in violence just hours before. I needed oxygen and wide open spaces to breathe freely.

"God, give me a sign," I prayed silently in the car. "Take me to a safe place. Help me to learn to break my addiction and release my obsession with The Enemy."

The fading paint on the old house we were about to enter seemed like a sign from God that old could be new and different, that I could change and grow.

Post-traumatic stress was forever. It was coming home to rest like the rocks on the shoreline that were pounded relentlessly by the surf and reshaped each season by rain and sand. I, too, would be different. This time, I was determined to be strong and steadfast.

I was in a daze, but began talking in my manic voice about why this time I was done with him. I could not get to this safe place on my own. I was too out of focus with reality.

It was quiet when we arrived, dark and still in the middle of a cool damp January night. I felt small, as if what was happening to me would go unnoticed, like the women inside. I related to them immediately; alone, but not. This must be where I should be. Would I admit it to myself?

FRIENDSHIP

My friend would never have taken me to this shelter if she did not think I needed the protection. She was a former school teacher, methodical in what she did. "I made a lot of phone calls for you," she said, with a look of fear on her face. "I've thought many times this would happen to you."

She was no fool. She had been preparing herself for tonight. She was a single mother with two teenage boys, and I had put her in a precarious position with this rescue. I desperately needed the responsible type, someone to take the helm. She was a person who clearly read maps and charted courses in her own life.

She had listened to some of my stories about this relationship, mostly with no comment. She had known abuse herself, but never really talked about it.

"Why do you think you keep going back to him?" she asked once.

"I don't know." I had no answer for her. I could not say it was love addiction.

If she judged me, I was not aware of it. Yes, I could have done something sooner, but I usually had to be scared to death to do the right thing. If I feared for my life, I made a change. This might have been one of those times.

She followed me to the door and then left quickly after a brief introduction. She had set me up for a full thirty-day stay. She left without a goodbye or a good luck.

THE SOJOURNER CENTER

The Sojourner Center was secluded in downtown Phoenix to protect the women it took in. It was not far from the golden dome of the state capital of Arizona. The efficient staff and this facility were at the mercy of state funding. The offering was limited.

"Welcome to the Sojourner Center," the intake woman said with a smile.

I responded with a weak nod and apprehension in my body language. Was this a safe place? Was I was willing to surrender and ask for help?

"Thank you, I guess."

"Three weeks or more is the best program," she continued.

"I cannot make that commitment. I'm not prepared to do that," I blurted out.

I continued to tread water and wait for the next thing to happen. I asked myself what was God's plan for me.

"I am really not one of them. You will be wasting a bed if you keep me here." I was sure I was going to be okay if I just had time to breathe and think.

My entrenched denial was the water coming up over my ears while I was drowning. I had been through a lot in my life. This was just another hard toss to the beach. I would get through this with my friends and family.

The woman behind the desk smiled and listened. She was way ahead of me. "You will be safe and your food, clothing and counseling will be provided," she promised. "You will begin to trust again with help from the staff, who will guide you."

I could not grasp how much help I might receive there or how much better I would be if I listened to her and trusted my journey with this place. My free spirit wanted freedom. My desperate need to break out and be my own person emerged again.

She motioned to a small, dark room in the back of the house where I would sleep, since I was getting the last bed. A small single cot, pressed against the back wall in a room with four sleeping girls, was waiting for me. She handed me a pile of faded towels, a pair of worn pajamas and a pillow I could do without. It was flat and useless, but I took it to be polite. I was always polite.

She did not blink at my angst and signs that I might be trying to jump ship. She ignored my apprehension about participating. The holiday season was a busy time for shelters. She was offering me a gift and expected me to be grateful. She was kind and gentle, yet straightforward and firm. She had worked with tough sailors before and used her knowledge from those experiences with me, too.

My swollen face was uncomfortable and my stitched head throbbed even harder than it had in the emergency room. I needed my own shower, my own bed, but I reluctantly accepted these accommodations. I had no other option. My friend was gone. I resigned myself to this quiet desperation and asked God for help.

DORM LIFE

Dorm life with other women was foreign to me. I had lived alone for more than twenty years and was used to my privacy and my loneliness. I pleaded silently in prayer, "God help me to be grateful—grateful to be alive, grateful to be safe for the night, grateful to have someone care for me and grateful for the shower I desperately need."

The hardest part of using their old bathroom, with its torn and cold linoleum floors, was facing myself in the small broken mirror. Before I undressed, I saw my sad reflection. The matted bunch of hair was more than I could bear. It was painful to see. I looked away. I remembered the nurse telling me, "You cannot wash your hair for ten days. The wound is large and needs to close and dry."

After I changed, I glanced back at the mirror with sad eyes. My image was a brutal reminder of just how low I sank before I was willing to ask for help and to change. How had it come to this?

I loved doing my hair. This no-wash plan would add to my shame as I saw more of my shine go away with ten days of dirty hair. I was a victim of domestic violence but I did not want to admit it. I prided myself on looking impeccable whenever I went out. My new look would be a daily reminder that the Enemy still controlled me. The shaved part of my head and the blue stitches punctuated the night and added to the painful reflection in that well-worn mirror.

I was angry with no way to vent. Could I close my eyes and sleep that night with this anger, even though I desperately needed sleep? My manic mind was running wild. It was as if I had opened all the sails, but kept pulling back.

Night Thoughts

I was angry at the Enemy for all he had done to me and for all I had allowed to happen between us. I felt sorry for myself and was afraid of where I had been. The images were a sad state shown in my distant eyes. I fell back into the dark hole of depression. It seemed impossible that night for me to move ahead and find hope.

I found myself fearful again as I laid there in the stillness. The outside street was a dark lake with a moonlit heaven as the street light shone in a small cracked window. It felt eerie to me in my loneliness. I was awake in a crowded room of strange women who were asleep when I arrived. I questioned who they were and if I knew any of them.

What happened to them? How did they finally end up here? Will this be the last time for them? Will this be the last time for me? I asked myself, expecting a sign, an answer. Did I subconsciously plan to be here? I pondered further. Is this what it takes for me?

The message was clear. I felt it deep in my soul. Deal with your anger and addiction now, before they kill you.

I prayed in a weak voice, "Please God; help me to see the similarities and not the differences with my new 'sisterhood.' Help me to believe we walk a similar path and keep me from denial. Help me to see that we can help each other somehow, someway."

All these questions, and my prayers, came down to my being willing to admit I was sick, to stop fighting and to accept I needed help. My life would get better only after I took the action necessary to make changes and bring some calm to my life.

My ego was holding me back. My low self-esteem was pushing me further into the sand as a part of me readied to dissolve these issues. *Will they become part of the shore's debris? If I stop the fight and surrender completely will I live, sail and conquer the biggest swells? Will I look back and reflect on how I not only survived the storm, but thrived in the rushing tide?*

THE ESCAPE

I found no comfort here. I was not willing to make it my home for thirty days. I could not close my eyes and sleep. When I did, I saw the Enemy's leering face, a face I could not eliminate from my thoughts. He controlled me still. I was very angry.

As I laid there, I thought about my soft warm bed, even though the thick, red bloodstains on the white wool blanket and the hand-woven rug came back into view. My rug had been woven together with love and kindness by a gentle weaver. *Will I eventually destroy them when I return home? Will I rid myself of all reminders of this night? Will I emerge from this dark night and shake off the Enemy for the last time?*

I needed to feel my blanket's warmth one more time. I needed that same feeling I once had from being comforted by warm sand on my back as I basked in the sunshine on a summer's day at Lake Michigan long ago.

Where would I find peace and an ebb and flow to my life?

"God help me keep the faith and move forward," I prayed. Is escaping this place a part of that process or a step back?

I shut my eyes. Visions of the beauty of the Sand Dunes beach near where I grew up surrounded me. The glow from the shore of the sun setting to the west down Lake Michigan offered peace to soothe my aching heart.

After a restless struggle, I crawled out of the bed and approached the woman at the front desk. She had her head down in her work.

"I need to leave. I am out of place here. May I use your phone?" My excuse had been repeated by other women in my circumstance.

She had heard it many times, but still tried to discourage me. "You're not giving our program a chance. Asking to leave now is hurting your chances to be free. Please reconsider; give this until tomorrow morning."

But in the end, she stepped back. Although my decision was unacceptable to her, she agreed it was not my time for her facility. I could not accept her help. She said no more, and with a concerned look, reluctantly handed me the phone.

"I cannot stay," I continued my plea. "I don't feel at home here. I have to go to a friend's house."

I was obsessed with the idea of getting back to Scottsdale. No one could convince me of the possible problems ahead or that I was sailing aimlessly. I could not see the warning signs of post-traumatic stress, depression or isolation that were all around me.

I called an older gentleman I knew from my church to pick me up. He was a comfort to me. He asked only a few questions, even though I disturbed him in the middle of the night.

The thirty minutes it took for him to come from Scottsdale to Phoenix to pick me up seemed like an eternity. The clock on the wall moved very slowly. With the woman at the desk watching me curiously, I waited like a wounded duck in a pond knowing a hunter was in the woods. I was also on high alert. I hoped the other women there had not heard my call. It was not fair to them.

The woman at the desk did not openly judge me. Her choice to give me some respect by going about her business while I waited, made me grateful. She obviously felt that I should not be leaving her facility, but did not insist on my staying at the center.

She had spent her career trying to help women like me. Had she been a victim of abuse herself? She wanted me to be one of her success stories. How did she feel about not having that chance? Her life was fixing the broken wings on the seagulls left damaged on the beach, but this one did not let her come closer.

What was holding me back? Why could I not receive her kindness?

My friend arrived and waited in the car in the dark at the end of the drive, but I knew it was him. I left the Sojourner Center with no real goodbye, just a quick thank you. I walked quickly to his car and jumped in the front seat. He barely looked at me.

"Hi," I said sheepishly.

We talked very little as he drove us to his small condo in Scottsdale. He had always liked me as a person and enjoyed my company, but during that dark night ride he was saddened. I knew it by his silence. I sensed it in the air as if a storm was brewing at sea. I needed to run for shelter on the beach.

"Are you going to be okay?" he finally blurted out.

"I am. This time will be different. I know it."

He did not respond.

I was considered attractive and intelligent. Why was I addicted to abusive men? Why do the nice guys finish last? Why do the dishonest charmers often suck in well-educated, successful women to years of abuse? I had no answers.

Although I was using my friend, in a way, I believed I had no choice. "Please God; allow me someday to return the favor," I prayed silently. I had made a decision and he was the one to rescue me. I was not proud of using my friend, but it was the only way I knew how to ask for help. I was too weak for anything else. I trusted him.

"Please God, forgive me for this selfishness. Guide me on a safer course," I whispered under my breath.

We went back to his condo in downtown Scottsdale, near where I lived. I slept on his couch that night, talking very little about what had happened. The next morning, he reluctantly drove me home. The fear of what had happened came over me as I opened the door and saw my bloody handprints on the back of the door. The reality of what transpired the night before began to settle in for me.

Moving Ahead

There is no perfect way to rise out of abuse and only a few right ways to do much about it. My therapist's words echoed in my brain. I'd had counseling several different times in my life, and now I was back into it—this time to deal with the effects of abuse. Would I take action now that I was forced to end this relationship? Would I despair all day? I began to forgive myself in order to get well. Forgiving the Enemy would have to come later.

My individual therapy was already in place. To continue with it would be a journey to some kind of closure. I made a commitment to our sessions and to accept responsibility for my life. Although overwhelmed at first, I knew therapy would help me immensely. I had done all of this in my earlier recovery. I knew it worked. I would find my faith again in God and mankind. I had to.

My first move was to seek validation for what happened to me by going back to the therapist I had been talking to about this relationship. Even though I had not been forthcoming in the past, she was someone who would understand and support me. Her attitude was paramount to my recovery.

"Please accept me again?" I asked her the first day. "I will be totally honest this time. I have a lot to tell you."

She just smiled and nodded.

To be accepted by someone willing and trustworthy was the beginning of real healing for me. She became my confidante. We shared a history of what it meant to feel less than; to feel insecure when the rest of the world saw us as confidant and strong. I began to open up more than I ever had with her, by not holding back the smaller details.

She suggested group therapy for more healing work. "You're going to recover one day at a time," she said. "just like you did in sobriety."

This was my safety net along the shore, my hidden cove of protection from the wind and blowing sand. My next decision included group therapy. I had heard about the Chrysalis Center's out-patient program in downtown Phoenix, and I made the call.

My second challenge was to work the recovery program she suggested at the Chrysalis Center. Their focus was on life-changing ideas in healing from trauma and violence. Self-love was the message that came through loud and clear. I was receptive to learning about the other women. I was not alone.

I began my journey courageously, even though I had lost my way when love addiction took over my psyche. The post traumatic stress had begun to grow, but things were improving with understanding and knowledge from this program.

"God guide me to get back my strength and to feel real again," I prayed.

My ego needed to be checked at the door when I entered group. I held a secret I was ashamed to share in earlier therapy, but now I desperately needed to discover why love addiction had taken me to these depths. I could not let it happen again. Healing was my main objective. I listened to the group leader and the other women. It was a necessary two-way street. I knew to no longer hide in isolation.

My final plan of action was to not allow anyone to enable me. I was the only one responsible for my start to good health. I consciously chose not to allow anyone to rescue me and tell me it was okay.

It was not acceptable for my friends to walk on eggshells around me. I needed them to be themselves, caring and brutally honest. I had many reasons to take a hard look at my reality and make changes. I found myself making my way up stream.

WITH POST TRAUMATIC STRESS

An important part of healing for me was to not avoid the memory of the event. I worked to remember as much as I could, as soon as possible, despite the difficulty.

"Try to understand why there are outbursts of anger in your daily life," my therapist suggested, "and why you're not sleeping through the night," she continued. "Why you're having difficulty concentrating and finishing projects."

My stress and anxiety were chronic. My depression was due to fear, shame and guilt. A crucial part of my recovery had begun weeks earlier at the Sojourner Center with small acts of kindness. I was beginning to appreciate the stepping stones.

"Do not deny what is happening," our group therapist insisted. "Your experience is a large part of your survival and will lead to your thriving later in life."

I learned memory and traumatic stress become the yin and yang. After many sessions, I also understood experiencing trauma was harmful physically, mentally, emotionally and spiritually.

Since I had been wounded before in earlier relationships, and damaged from prior traumas such as a car accident, post-traumatic stress was a big part of my life. I embraced the accepted definition of post traumatic stress as "outside the range of usual human experience and markedly distressing."

Going to the white fog at the peak of the assault was one part of post-traumatic stress I used to my advantage. It was a way of preparing me to "numb" the awareness. Because of the intense fear, helplessness and estrangement I felt along with the horror of the event, I immediately avoided recollection. By not recalling my story, it would become a physical reminder in illness. My high-anxiety element of stress had to be addressed immediately. The trauma was physically and visibly apparent; none of what happened could be hidden. It was time to confront the truth.

I was near death inside; just as I was near death outside the night I was taken to the emergency room and to the Sojourner Center. I was losing myself and all I believed in. I was a lost soul, but I was not forgotten.

THE TERROR IN PTS

*You gain strength, courage, and confidence by every experience
in which you really stop to look fear in the face.*
Eleanor Roosevelt

STARTING PTS

Any loud sound sent chills down my spine. Having my hair touched by a stranger was unnerving, so I trimmed it myself. I tried to fight back the terror, but it was futile. I was trapped in my own mind like a rat in the hull of an old ship.
Just as I was frozen in time on the floor of my bedroom the night of the assault, I was motionless in much of what I did.

"Am I unconscious, am I living outside of myself? Help me, God," I prayed.

Since I endured the pain and humiliation of being brutally attacked by a man I had trusted too many times, my trust level was nil. *What is happening to me? I can't get free of him and get back to my old self.*

The dead-bolted patio door lock that could not be undone, easily closed in on me, forcing a captive situation. I had installed that lock myself. My life was out of control.

God had taken me to the white fog, that state of peace that froze me in time; my safety net. I wanted that fog that settled in my subconscious to protect me again from my fear and pain.

"Please, God, I feel hopeless. Give me the faith to hold on," I prayed. But exhaustion came quickly. I fought hard for a long, long time, and was wet with musty sweat when the Enemy attacked me. I woke from my nightmares in that same state. I felt the blood from my head gash wash over my face again and again. I was overwhelmed and existing purely on adrenalin.

The back of my head felt achy for a long time, as if it would require another trip to the emergency room. "Dear God, what will I need, what should I do?" I murmured, as sadness came.

The deep red-blue bruises that spotted my arms and legs showed the topography of that night for about a week. They only added to the memories of what could have been. The scratches and punctures danced across my face and neck like red highways on a map sketched out in a hurry. They eventually healed and could be hidden with make-up, but I knew they were there and they carried shame. To help forget the pain, I searched for its purpose in prayer and time with my thoughts.

The white fog from the assault changed to a haze of sadness that slowly began to lift. My conscious brain freed me with some clarity a little each day. I brushed away what had felt like gritty sand on my skin that night; now I had to brush away the shame. The dust from the carpet had been ground into my face. I would not allow shame to do the same. I slowly pushed myself along, as the chill of the incident set in. I shivered often as the shock set in.

Please God protect me. The shield of adrenaline rush buffered me often from possible hyperventilation. A state of heightened alert for danger was now mine. Like the eerie warning sirens heard at sea, I screamed out deep in my soul. The emotional pain disguised as longtime fatigue was now exhaustion. I had never experienced such terror, such fear for my life and shaking, that would take a lot of time to overcome. I was almost non-functioning. I was truly wounded.

The possibility of recovery sounded an alarm in me far greater than ever I could have imagined. Although I still had antagonistic feelings for the Enemy, my focus was now on my mental and emotional well-being. My grasp of what had transpired that awful night was weak, but growing. I was extremely anxious to learn more to help in my recovery.

The abuse of the relationship and the choices I made would flash before me. The sight of my fresh red blood on the back of my front door, my hands and my robe as I tried to exit my condo had not only enhanced the images of the beating, but were indelibly etched in my memory. My breath was quick and short when I recalled those visuals. The tenseness in my chest returned when the stress of the night came back to me.

I disconnected emotionally as if it weren't real. My two years of abuse and trauma with this person were written very clearly and heavily with those bloody hand prints. My image in the mirror near the door told me I had been stuck in this type of danger for a long time. How was I going to get out of post-traumatic stress? Would it be easier than leaving that captive relationship, or would it be harder?

My fear released adrenaline. It rushed through me as I escaped my condo to the stairwell outside. It would serve me well again in the battle with the aftermath of trauma. The Enemy left me behind but now I was out front running alone and I would make it. There was a tidal wave of emotion that often did not allow me time to breathe, but I kept going. My faith in God was there for me.

Chaos was familiar to me; fear was a part of my persona. Stress controlled my every move. *God, I accept I cannot change things.* These were painful thoughts.

With a large head-wound that would take weeks to close, the physical damage went deep. I was dismantled like an old house weathering away on the beach, but I would heal.

The emotional scars that tied me to the Enemy seemed endless. The fighting in my bedroom that night proved intense and passionate in a bizarre kind of way—a sexual, violent way— and in a way that showed the senselessness of our relationship. I was haunted by those memories.

Similar to the panic of being aboard a sinking ship with nowhere to go, I had visions of a fierce encounter with a shark. The inequities of my physical and mental strength made life seem unfair. "I must survive. He wanted to save face and keep his power when he used coercive control over me. Now I need to do the same," I told my therapist.

Nothing with us had been steady. I never found a reprieve with him, I had to find it now, and a way to beat this menacing predator... PTS. I was irritable and on edge most of the time. It had to stop. This horrible life-threatening culmination of my relationship with the Enemy had to cease or I was going to crack.

BUILDING PTS

I am angry. I am hurt and sad. I was all of those things and more, but admitted to very little and to my part in the beginning. I was just grateful to be a survivor.

This abusive relationship had been a lot of wasted time and energy. I was slowly learning to forgive myself so I could heal completely.

"Help me take the guilt and shame away," I begged my therapist. "I have many sleepless nights and I am feeling physically ill."

I could not predict how this would play out. Love addiction had made me do crazy and dangerous things. I admitted that now. It was a start. I did not want to continue down that path of destruction, but it was not going to end abruptly.

Disdain hung in the air around me while I remembered that my warm blood slowly moved across my face. I could not remember entering my room or being on the bed. The evidence was locked in my memory.

I have to remember what happened here, I cried frantically in the night. *God, release me somehow.* I prayed the answers would surface to help my recovery. I was very angry and not in control of my emotions. I knew I had a long way to go but that I needed to keep the faith.

There had been a lot of evidence in the room that night with blood splatters across the white walls. The vision of it kept coming back to me. The bloodshed of that battle washed over me as I revisited it in nightmares. The white area rug that was splattered in red blood that night had to be destroyed. I loved that rug, but it had to go.

I keep seeing the blood when I close my eyes.

My soft nightgown had been peppered with blood spots and torn across the front in many places from this rampage of hate. It symbolized all that was wrong with the relationship. It was a dreadful reminder of what we had and didn't have.

"I am disgusted for being in this position and for staying in it so long," I told God in a dark hour. "Please help me."

I stressed about sharing the details with anyone for fear of my shame-based feelings. Thus began my self-blame on steroids and a long journey back to myself.

"Why do I not remember all of what happened?" I pondered in therapy. "Why are some details not clear to me? Is God protecting me? Will this temporary amnesia help me? Was I so detached that I was not really alive?" I asked further.

The Enemy's anger had been hurled at me as if it were a storm at sea coming out of nowhere and at an unpredictable speed. Just as the eeriest sounds pierce the night on a quiet lake, my body and mind were now on high alert for an unexpected turn that could be disastrous, maybe deadly. This was PTS and this was where I was. My physical being was held taut from stress.

I now lived overwhelmed and disorganized from the shear fear that post-traumatic stress produced in me. With tightness in my chest and shortness of breath, I often felt a suffocating sensation. My whole being was often shut off from life like a door slammed shut. The aches and pains were daily nuisances.

I feel like a small goldfish sealed in plastic, one you win at the fair for a dime.

I prayed for God's Grace. I was determined to break free from the post-traumatic stress that engulfed me. I searched my conscious brain for answers as to what it was and how to deal with it. I was moving on with my life at a snail's pace.

THE SHOCK SET-IN

"Did I do this final act on purpose? Was I searching for this last conflict?" I asked God in a quiet moment. "Why was I reckless? Why was I not attentive to my safety?" I continued in my searching. "How will I pay for this decision?"

The answers came in God's time. I followed my heart and prayed daily, morning and night. *Please God; fill me with your grace.*

My mind held on to angry thoughts and harsh memories. I dreaded what life might have in store for me with post-traumatic stress if I did not forgive him or myself. This had to change for me to heal.

Please God, there can be no more outbursts of anger. I am scaring myself.

Fight back, but don't take revenge, was the path God showed me and the one I took. There was no other way. *Do not pursue him in a court of public opinion,* was part of the message from God and a sign to move on.

I have found forgiveness in my heart. I can move on. Post-traumatic stress will not be allowed to devour me. I choose to fight back.

Too often I ventured through life without asking for help. It was dangerous and truly risky behavior. Alienation was never the best answer, but I chose it just the same. My night of terror was still vivid. Death at the hands of my perpetrator had been possible; it happens to women every few minutes, every day in our country. My life could have ended in a split second. The shock of that reality glared at me.

In the months that followed this assault, the initial shock set in. I experienced intense emotions. The Enemy had crossed the line and taken me with him. My feelings of helplessness, self-pity and self-loathing would not leave me any time soon. I was emotionally spent and empty, fighting a last-ditch effort to thrive as a survivor.

Overwhelmed with the smallest change in my environment, and startled by the slightest noise, I was on high alert all the time. I created difficulties in my personal and business life by being less productive and attentive to my needs. Everything was magnified; no task was easy.

I had problems dealing with the public, which used to be so easy for me. I raged internally, was short with people and gave terse answers. I trusted no one at first glance. Depression was near. I thanked God each night for pulling me through this horrific experience long before I could see it happening.

I rarely spoke to anyone about what happened to me, both out of the fear of having to tell my story again and their just being stunned by it all. I lost interest in my recovery for quite some time. Although sharing my story eventually helped me slowly release my fearful thoughts, doing so did not come easily for me.

I did not understand myself, maybe I never had. I was insecure about my decisions. My mind could not shut down. I doubted myself at every turn. There was no peace for me. It was as if a crank had been turned on inside me, winding tighter and tighter. I found it extremely difficult to concentrate.

Crazily trying to relive the event as much as I could, and record those thoughts in my journal, I found many loose ends that had no explanation.

"My notes make no sense. I am scattered and the entries are not even readable most of the time," I told the lead therapist in group.

My seemingly futile counseling sessions frustrated me. I was alone and drifting further from the shore. There was no beacon of light in my midst.

How will I know what really happened to me? How am I going to learn the details to help myself in court? Who will get me justice?

I was now talking incessantly about the assault in the group sessions, with no emotion behind the words. My thoughts ran in circles.

PROCESSING EMOTIONS

As I began to disconnect from the Enemy, I was like the proverbial buoy bouncing aimlessly in the water. I continued to process my emotions by expressing myself in my journal.

I hate what happened to me. I hate that I allowed myself to get into this position. I hate what he did to me and what I did to myself.

I rode my words like waves heaving endlessly to the shore. I was an abandoned craft adrift in the water tossed by the waves.

During this period of high emotion, I kept thinking there was someone stalking me. I feared I was not alone, and was unsafe.

"Who's there?" I would ask at the door.

I believed that someone would attack and beat me. Extreme anxiety had set in. I napped intermittently and slept very little, just under the surface. I was aware of most things around me, due to my hyper-vigilance.

"Did you hear anything last night in the courtyard?" I asked my neighbor.

"No." She answered with trepidation, hearing exhaustion in my voice.

Initially, I moved from the sub-basement apartment where the assault took place to a condo a few miles away. I barricaded myself behind its security wrought iron fence. I felt a little safer with the locked gates versus the open walkways of the other place.

Will I feel safe? Is the gate locking only an illusion of safety?

My blood pressure rose. I could feel it pumping in my head. My heart beat as fast as the rush of the copper falls at Tahquamenon I remembered from childhood. I was on high alert for danger, twitching at times for no reason.

"The lock opening on the outside of the courtyard gate unnerves me," I told my new neighbor. "Does it feel safe in here for you?"

"Safe to a point, but nothing is one hundred percent," she said.

"I have a sense of great loss for a peaceful life; like what we would find in a small town," I said in sadness. "I grew up in a small town."

I found it hard to believe I would ever have that life again. I kept to myself, letting my new neighbor get to know only a little about me. I was not ready to trust. I was easily startled, but I knew I had to keep moving forward and take care of myself by doing what I needed to do to feel safe. Staying behind closed doors helped.

I will try to not to be alarmed by noises in the street or sirens and activity at night. I have chosen to live alone in my new condo.

Believing that positive affirmations would help me, I wrote this mantra each day.

This was my new normal. My isolation and cautious behavior were how I lived and survived. Exhaustion ruled every part of my being.

"This small life I now have is okay with me. I accept it as an opportunity to find myself," I told my therapist, even when I did not believe it myself.

I got to know loneliness at a deeper level. I had lived alone for many years and was not afraid by nature. But now this tension was upsetting my usual habits. I worked to make a home for myself at the new place and believed it could be a step forward. I pledged to take each day as it came. I signed the lease with the intention of living there for a long time. My goal was to begin to process my emotions thoroughly and move on.

Disconnecting Memory from Feelings

Being afraid and never making plans to be out after dark gave my post-traumatic stress permission to settle in. I obsessed on repeatedly checking the doors and windows, locks and hallways in my condo as a new routine.

"I want to be in a quiet, closed off environment to avoid sounds that startle me," I told my therapist. "My condo is a safe haven in a way, but it is not working for me all the time."

"You need to work at your meditation and believe that it will work for you," she suggested. "I will help you with it. It has worked for many of my clients."

With post-traumatic stress as my challenger, I worked at minimizing my memories of that relationship's violence through prayer and meditation. I had a God and I was going to use Him now. The loud sounds never totally left me, so I started with disconnecting my memory from my feelings in the meditation. I worked one day at a time just as I had done with my AA recovery. My therapist helped me talk it out, too, but I had to want this to happen. I had to have faith.

With both the criminal and civil trials taking place one after the other, anxiety overwhelmed my life. I relived everything over and over to the point of exhaustion.

What was my part? What could I have done to stop the violence sooner? How did all of this change me as a person?

I was in preparation for my victim's statement at trial. I set this project aside several times so I could be clear about it and not so emotional. I could not function with it raw all the time.

I prepared myself mentally and emotionally for the trial by my journaling. I visualized myself reading the statement and prayed about what would transpire. I often found myself disconnected from the memory when I needed it because I had stuffed my feelings for so long. It was the post-traumatic stress at work. I had met quite the foe. Because I had been in therapy for many months, the trauma was at the forefront of my mind, but the emotions were still deeply hidden. It had been so long since I cried I could hardly remember what that purging felt like and how much it soothed the soul. The nightmare of being hunted down by him and stalked relentlessly over two years was often my picture show when I closed my eyes at night.

"I can rarely find relief except with moments of prayer and meditation or times out for a walk," I wrote in that statement. "My sanity has been derailed and I have been cheated of any semblance of peace."

As much as I wanted him out of my life, he was still there, disturbing me and controlling me, and would be until the trials were over and I could put this part to rest.

FACING AND FEELING EMOTIONS

Every night the nightmares came. For a long time sleep escaped me until an hour or two before my alarm sounded, as fear crept over me like a dark shadow in the room. Anger appeared easily, as if it belonged to me.

One nightmare was a reenactment of my car repeatedly being damaged by tire slashes. With a small, sharp knife, maybe a carpet knife, this had occurred several times. It was him doing it in the nightmare, even though he had always denied it to me, and the police could never prove who did it. It was his silhouette in one of his fancy suits that would haunt me for a long time, doing damage to me and my things.

The flashbacks would also come when I was awake, when I was in a location that reminded me of that abusive life. They came while driving by the corner where the assault occurred. They surfaced when entering the mall area across the street from where I hid my car, because I had dealt with vandalism too many times. I feared the emergency entrance of the hospital where I was stitched up. It was across the street from the library that I frequented. I often avoided going, even when I wanted to be there, or I parked blocks away in order to not see the hospital.

Flashbacks of beatings encompassed my thoughts like an intense storm of waves pounding against a large window at the helm of a ship. There was no shield to subdue the sound. The fear was often overpowering and I would shake because of it.

I'm a zombie of my own making, afraid of my thoughts. I feel a sense of great loss. I grieve for a life I never had. My mental health is deteriorating with the stress.

"I have known grief and loss before, with the death of my sister, and my good friend many years ago. But this is a new kind of loss," I shared in therapy. "It is making a deep hole in me."

"This feeling of hopelessness, when the chaos and anger collide, will help you see the terror in your mind's eye," my therapist assured me. "This will help you. The cruelty went deep to your soul; it will take time."

I cannot stop the repetition of the image or the reminders of the assault, but eventually I will. I know I will, I assured myself, as similar violence occurred on the news.

I continued to put myself in harm's way with other unworthy men. I subconsciously reenacted the crime with hidden hopes of a release. I could not stop doing this, believing I was trying to find answers. I physically suffered within my body and soul, causing pain that related to nothing that was diagnosed. It was an ache that was like no other and one that felt like it would never leave. My neck pain increased with the stress and my fingertips were usually numb in the morning. My neck cracked and popped with very little movement.

Stress hormones played a vital role in my deepening the memory of the incident. They ramped up every aspect of the aftermath of trauma. Rather than verbalizing the story, I acted out with anger and felt it in my bones. I overreacted to situations and could not see things clearly. Fear was my constant companion. In my heart, I knew I had to face and feel the emotions.

GRADUALLY OVER TIME

"The Enemy is not going to control my life any longer," I announced to my therapist after many months. "I am going to take back my life and totally move on from all of this."

Even though I was still careless in my behavior and decisions, I was now willing to defy the odds about what was almost physically impossible for me. I went out for evenings alone to the mall or a movie, angrily trying to prove I was not mentally ill or living in fear. Sometimes I returned home in a debilitating state.

Defiant at times, with my newfound courage, I took over my body, mind and spirit as best I could. I pushed myself farther and farther into a depression because the situation was so difficult.

I am out of sorts. I am powerless. My hands and feet are tied by an imaginary rope that confines me. It is hard to predict the moments of tension surfacing. When will I know what to do or how to handle things?

To heal, recover and move on meant I had to keep the faith that each day would be better than the day before. My problems kept persisting, but I was willing to learn the lesson I needed.

I will be open and honest about what is going on with me. I want to heal.

Gradually, I surrendered to the process of recovery for the anxiety called post-traumatic stress. I admitted that the Enemy and I were two people who should have never been in each other's lives except to learn our truth. Love addiction was my truth. I believed we crossed paths only so the life lessons God needed to teach me could occur and my healing and recovery could begin. There was no other way but this way and I now accepted that fact.

In my ongoing therapy I allowed myself to experience the event fully and remember more than I had initially. I no longer avoided scenes that were reminders. I no longer shunned people who could trigger anything. I stood taller and wider to the possibilities of healing and recovering.

I was now willing to re-experience the event with others and my therapist so I could heal. Although there was anxiety for a long time, and an emotional arousal I did not anticipate, I persevered. I shared my story in my group, with others on my path.

This piece of my life happened so I could get to the other side of my struggle with love addiction and chaos. In some ways, it brought out the worst of me and simultaneously got me to seek the best for myself. It helped me take a look at the secrets in my life, my addiction and my fear of abandonment. This relationship taught me many lessons, and for that I am grateful. I was now on an endless path of healing and recovery.

DISCONNECTION

There are no hopeless situations;
there are only people who have grown hopeless about them.
William Barclay

HEALING

L ike the slow, careless rolls of the waves on the beach I remembered from my childhood near Lake Michigan, fear was overtaking me those first few days after the assault.

"My healing has not yet begun," I told my therapist. "I have nothing to shield my mental anguish. I pray for God to touch my heart."

"It is easy to assume healing will begin when the abuser is gone, but that is not true," she began. "Many traumatized women seek drugs and alcohol to take away the pain, to help alleviate the nightmares and the fear that lives within them. We know these are not options for you."

I held on to her comments. My post-traumatic stress brought anxiety and chest pain. I recognized these symptoms as mental health issues and possibly imagined pain or unnecessary anguish.

"Regardless of the relationship situation you were in, you likely know someone else who has shared your experience," she suggested. "I have great admiration for those who have walked beyond their trauma. You can be one of those, too."

I appreciated her sharing hope with me. A hunger for answers to many questions buoyed up in me when I listened to her.

Why do I think I am different? I am trying to learn why I do certain things. I want to learn to do those things better the next time. What is it about abuse and anger and addiction that binds me to abused women?

Post-traumatic stress was a ticking time bomb behind my forced smile. I fought to find my rhythm, my sync, my natural flow. Going to my office each day was difficult. I wore my hair up over the stitches and repeatedly went to the bathroom to check myself. I was preoccupied with my looks. My dirty hair consumed me.

I knew my patience and faith were critical at this stage, yet so hard to find as I anticipated the next big wave of pain. I would then have to step outside and get a breath of fresh air and let the sun hit my face to calm me down.

"Are you okay?" a friend asked one day, as I sat with my head in my hands. "You look so pale, not like yourself."

"I am okay, really. I just need more sleep. Work and school is a lot sometimes."

Like the surfer at sunrise vying for that first perfect ride, I fought every morning to hide the shaved part of my head adorned with blue stitches. Blue, so the doctor could find them and remove them later. Blue, like the deep sadness I was drowning in. I longed to dismantle the pain as the sun came up to warm my soul. I held onto my thoughts for a good ride each day. My therapist was always just a phone call away.

When stressed, I recalled going to her small office in downtown Scottsdale. Remembering her many framed quotes and pictures helped to set my mind in a calming mood. I slowed down after entering my thoughts. She always leaned in when she greeted me and offered a gentle hand and soothing instrumental music. She practiced yoga and meditation, too; opening a kinship. She kept her office only slightly cluttered. It had the nice feel of home.

"You cannot find solace by escaping your reality, as you did with drinking over failed marriages and unhappy life decisions," she stated in our next session just days later. "We will work together to help you reach out to people again."

"I am lonely and sad even with my friends. I am distant from family; they are many miles away," I added. "My conversations at work are only small guarded attempts to connect to some of the women there. I like those women a lot and don't understand it."

The wall around me was slowly breaking away. A couple of women in my office had walked in my shoes. They recognized the signs and reached out to me. I threw off anchor lines and accepted some invitations to share a sandwich across the street from the office. I felt better when I did. Thank God they could see me.

By not running away from them, my freedom from captivity began. My shell was reflective of my life, jagged and slightly fractured. But I was opening up now by writing in my journal. Blunt and honest and purging for the truth, I was sharing more in therapy about my love addiction and how much it had affected my life.

"A change of priorities, a life with less responsibility is what you need," my therapist recommended. "A life with your AA women friends fulfills you. Reach out to them again."

She was right. This had worked for me in the past. It would again. I focused on my writing passion, too, and the spiritual life I desired and set out on a steadier course. My therapist's soft, reassuring voice echoed in my head. I visualized her understanding eyes and the peacefulness of her presence and how it accented everything we talked about and reinforced her trademark.

Disconnection was ever present, the defensive side of post-traumatic stress. I prayed for peace in my heart and challenged myself to stop short of anger and frustration. My commitment to look at the bigger picture when demanding clients caused stress at work moved me forward. I needed the position of realtor assistant until I was well enough to move on and use the Masters Degree I had miraculously earned during my two years in this abusive relationship.

Peace crept into my life and put me in a better place. The plan was to be cool under fire in my daily life. Like the sailor who lost communication and looked to the stars for guidance, my work in therapy helped me to find stillness and to begin to let go of anger.

EVOLVING

The domestic violence counseling in group therapy at the Chrysalis Center was challenging with my post-traumatic stress. My therapist suggested adding this element to my recovery even though it was a half-hour drive from my condo. Many times, I had to force myself to make the agonizing trip alone. The traffic was often heavy, but parking was good. There was no one to carpool with, so I asked God to help me stay positive and be grateful for this meeting, the people and the venue.

The facility was located on the second floor of an office building, not a cozy atmosphere. The furniture was stark and gray, as if an accountant had chosen it. I was uncomfortable and wished I was back in my therapist's warm office.

Who donated the place for us? Did the Chrysalis Center have any choice but to be here? There are no plants or warm art pieces on the wall. How odd.

Group therapy was essential to my healing. The pull of fantasy love was as strong as alcohol had been for me. The compulsive beckoning was the same. I wanted to quit, I had to quit, and I could not go back there.

"Most women who have been traumatized or abused cannot seek a new way of life alone. They must be shown the way," our group leader presented the first week.

She was a heavy woman and her chest heaved each time she spoke. She was determined; her round face lit up when she talked. Her smile was framed by unruly gray hair and she smelled of lavender. She wore neutrals like the décor. I liked her and thought lavender should be her color.

At this juncture, I became willing to take a harder look at my love addiction, which had almost cost me my life. I approached the group therapy with the thought of safety first; not just physical safety, but emotional and psychological safety, too. This was necessary to my overall well-being. I had no patience to peel away the layers beneath the anger. Too often I would quit before the healing took place, like when I first accepted my alcoholism.

By expressing my desires and needs honestly in my therapy and group sessions, and letting my feelings be known to those I trusted, I was on my way to winning. I sought God's help through prayer and meditation each morning.

Statistics said it would only be a matter of time before I would be looking for someone to pay attention to me or to be with me at any cost. For me to pick up where I had left off was extremely tempting, but I was determined to not return to my old destructive lifestyle. My faith continued to be tested. My existence had to change to a simpler life with close friends for lunch or a movie, or just a quiet evening alone reading or writing.

"Do you have any idea just how widespread the suffering really is out there in the world of dependency?" our leader questioned us, as we readied to say goodbye after eight difficult weeks. "You can be a model of hope for other women," she concluded.

God, I am willing to look at my part in all of this. I am a victim. I am not to blame for the abuse, but I still need to look constantly at the issues that plague me. My addiction to love and to chaos is very real. I can no longer avoid talking about it. Please help me to grow.

I said goodbye to the women at the Chrysalis Center with hope and trepidation. I wanted our paths to cross again as we carried our message forward. For some of us, that would happen, for others, maybe not. I looked forward to being of service in some way to God and to these women.

THE COALITION

I moved ahead on a course charted by God. I researched women's groups and found a support group with the Arizona Coalition against Domestic Violence (AZCADV). I signed up for their weekly email newsletter and followed their website. I wasn't quite ready to join them as a survivor speaker. I learned more about who I was and what I could do to help by reading the information they offered.

After a couple of months, I responded more openly with this group. I was willing to be a part of the give and take. I accepted the invitation for survivor speaker training and said I would volunteer. There would be no second chance for me to return from Death's door. Like a small boat lost in raging rapids on a river trip, I had spun out of control. I thanked God this group was ready to hear and accept my truth.

My symptoms were rampant and the destructive pattern was visible for a long time. My post-traumatic stress was powerful and dominated my life with high alerts and nightmares. Fear would not easily go away. But love, support and time with women on my journey helped heal my wounds.

In my nightmares, the lost were speaking to me. I learned from the survivor training session what not to do, a gift from those who had walked before me. By discussing the women's stories, I found balance in my own life. I worked to remain strong. I continued to journal each morning with the notes from the training. These reflections were invaluable.

"To seize alcohol to ease pain and escape a traumatic experience is not the answer," began my therapist in our last session.

"My recovery is over a decade long," I reminded her. "That part of my life is strong, but I am at a crossroads. There is a path that leads to more heartache if I do not seek my recovery in a new way," I said with determination. "The domestic violence sharing group will be good for me. I am ready to tell my story to help others understand."

Those words rang through my head often during those early months. I walked away from professional commitments to get sound in mind and spirit. Other obligations such as Toastmasters were set aside. I went inside myself and refocused on me and how my sharing would help me and others.

THE SUPER BOWL

When I did not cancel volunteering at the Super Bowl Experience just a few months after the assault, I was overwhelmed. Still fearful whenever anyone approached me, I believed I was alone on an island amongst many who could not see me. I couldn't reveal where I was emotionally even to my close friend, who was there with me, and I distanced myself from her that day. Stuck in my terror and fear, I was angry at the person inside me who could not get out.

To work well with kids at the amusement area for this national event was almost impossible. I hardly functioned. It was too soon after the assault. I was uncomfortable with the crowds. Even though there was an abundance of security, and I was with others on my team in a guarded area, I was uneasy and stayed only a few hours.

I walked away from that event and the opportunity to be a part of something big in the community. I lost hope. All those weeks of therapy had washed away in that one day. Post-traumatic stress had a powerful hold on me.

The devastating effects of the assault had taken hold. I would never be the same. Friends and family were already dismissing the incident. I started doubting myself as well. It was too painful for them, too foreign and too hard. I couldn't make it easier for them; it was my life.

"Am I alone in this? Do I have no choice in the matter? I hate to think that is the case," I asked my therapist after a restless night's sleep.

"You're not alone. There's help for you. It'll take time but it'll happen," she said.

My AA meetings were hard at first. I had to admit my secret. But the philosophy of the program was a solid part of my being. I had not disowned my recovery friends, and they had not left me. I had just not completely let them in to all my secrets about love addiction, and now I had to talk about post-traumatic stress, too. I felt a part of the program at a new level. Their acceptance was what I needed and received.

I embraced AA 12-Step Recovery by making amends to my friends. They had suffered too, by my actions, my lies. I went back with a new attitude that brought me closer to God every day. I was free of that old captivity. Just like struggling in a storm, all options were considered and a choice for survival was made.

GROWING

To learn more about myself, I simplified my life even further. I chose to have fewer people around me, selecting only the right people to share my new recovery journey. With little chaos to deal with, there was a vision of hope. I didn't accept every invitation that came my way, especially ones that would not be good conversation. Those simple steps of acceptance and forgiveness from my earlier AA recovery were still in place. They would serve me well again. I was a woman on the threshold of a new life. I desired a slow and quiet pace.

"Shed the old, and accept and welcome the new," my therapist suggested on our next visit. "Learn how much less you can get along with, so you have more time for yourself." Her call encouraged me to action.

We were winding down our time together. I was becoming open to the new plans God had in store for me. I signed up for a yoga class and committed to it with all my heart, going each week as well as practicing at home. It had been a long time since I practiced yoga. The women in class were about my age; I was not intimidated and started with a beginner's class.

"The risk of dependency and addiction is high for any survivor of trauma. Your entire existence is fluctuating with your emotions and your physical energy," my therapist presented in our last session. "The risk of falling back to where you came from is very high because you have suffered from other traumas as well."

Sadness, depression, alcoholism, trauma and abuse added to the pile of debris on the beach where I lived. She was talking about me. Falling back into that trap of denial and taking the wrong road that appeared to be the easier and softer way could happen.

"When these traumas mount up, they heighten your post-traumatic stress," she added.

"I have survived an unusual amount of trauma. I know I have anxiety." I accepted and confirmed her words. "With God's grace, I found a safety-net with my therapy group. I went to the depths of my soul to find a way to live fully, maybe for the first time in my life," I assured her. And myself.

Although on high alert, I began to learn further what to do and how to survive. Writing was a big part of my growth. It was cathartic for me and comforting in my grief for both my lifestyle changes and for my loss of security.

With over ten years of sobriety, I embraced my spirituality with even more daily prayer. Drinking was not an option. I sought ways to deal with everything, when necessary. I stayed close to my AA and Alanon women friends and listened to what they told me. Their listening ears and prayers sustained me. I did not isolate myself any longer.

"To face what God has in store for you, you only need to accept His will. Live your spiritual path with the deepest of gratitude," advised my AA sponsor. "Nothing is impossible."

She was right. I wrote that phrase in my gratitude journal every week. I broke out of my familiar pattern of destruction. I filtered nothing God sent my way and went to the bare bones. I took each day as it came. Like the mist of the sea that needs to rise, I, too, needed to move upward.

GOD

Once I allowed God's messages to come through by listening to my heart in daily meditation, I no longer needed to try to control my life. The Enemy was not my Higher Power anymore. He was removed from my psyche. I was getting to experience renewal. I removed my pride each day by asking for God's help, and I became more honest with them.

"Stop blaming yourself for what happened. Stop making yourself the scapegoat for a scenario you could not control," my AA sponsor said. "God's in charge."

"God has more lessons for me to learn. I really believe that. I am shedding my masks," I shared with her. "I deserve emotional freedom, too. Things are better."

This acknowledgement gave me some peace. I sought that little ray of hope that the next week I would be calmer and more open to ideas about how to live my life. Like the beacon of an old lighthouse, my need to change did not die. I prayed for God's grace, wanting the new and the old lives to be oceans apart.

I had lost myself once while being washed up in a sea of fear. But now, I could stop the wave of terror. I found the answer by maintaining hope with the words of encouragement from my AA meetings, my therapist and my sponsor and God. I radiated in the beauty and purpose of growing.

THRIVING

"The answer is not on the outside, but on the inside," my therapist repeated. "We will find your disconnection from life and connect to life again. You will know what it is to hope and thrive."

I was doing better with meeting new people and socializing after dark with my own friends. Her words kept ringing in my ears. Even with all I had learned in my therapy and group sessions, and knowing that God speaks to me through others, I was still struggling on occasion.

It was spring, a beautiful time of the year in Arizona; with perfect temperatures for blossoms everywhere. I prayed for this to be a sign of my new phase of life, too.

"I am a different person. I can be her, this new strong person," I told my therapist after weeks of doing some of what she suggested. "I am often a scared rabbit in a hole, peering out. I only venture out for basic survival needs when the coast is clear."

My isolation was smothering, even more so than during my abusive relationship. In my darkest moments, I heard God say, "Listen to your thoughts, hear My voice, feel your pain and live for yourself." I was reluctant to do it at first but I clung to my therapist's word: "Thrive."

All my life I tried to avoid being alone, yet here I was feeling it again. If I was going to push through, I had to work the basics. This was an emergency. I cringed at the thought of going down that road, but my therapist's office was a healing place and so was AA. Why did I fear this journey? Why did I not fully tell the truth until my back was up against the wall?

"This is hard work," she said often. "You have to want to not only survive but to thrive. You can do this; you are stronger than you think you are," she said, to keep me going.

"I want this. I truly do."

"Because addiction stifles growth and keeps you at an early stage of emotional development, you have to be vigilant," she said. "Until you are fully in recovery and truly ready, you do not recognize the severity of your situation."

I began to see my addiction to chaos and relationships as mental illness. Ending them permanently happened when I pledged to take the next step in my overall recovery; to stay the course no matter what waves came my way. I was getting stronger.

The teachings of my 12-Step AA recovery program and the blessings of life lessons were getting through to me now. My spiritual quest was opening. For this I was most grateful. I was poised to share my strength and hope with others and to stay long term in my AA recovery. I was ready to choose life fully.

Trials and Tribulations

Do the thing you fear and the death of fear is certain.
Ralph Waldo Emerson

Representation

There was no preparation for the criminal trial. The City Attorney was not available to meet with me before my day in court. He did not call. No meetings happened between us. He was too busy. I became a victim of the court.

I had expected a meeting to discuss what happened and what we were going to say and do to get a conviction. Hoping for some empathy and support, and an advocate, I assumed somebody in the City Attorney's Office would call. I didn't choose him, he was appointed by the court. My dislike for him grew as he neglected me and my case.

I called the Mayor's office about the City Attorney, envisioning a more helping hand from someone I knew had a reputation for caring for the community. He was outgoing and gregarious, a concerned leader.

I could not accept being a victim again. I vividly told my story to the Mayor's eager listening ear, including all the details I felt necessary to make my point. I wanted to participate as the victim. I wanted to see the Enemy convicted.

"I feel I'm being abused again. Is it because I know the intruder that I am being treated differently?" I asked. "Is it because it was a violent relationship for a long time?"

The Mayor acknowledged the ambivalent treatment by the City Attorney as if he had seen these dealings before. I began to see a pattern of what the City Attorney was like, even what he looked like as he proceeded in a stoic and methodical way.

"It is unacceptable that he hasn't called you," the Mayor said. "I am going over to the City Court office to speak to him. I would be very upset if my wife or daughter was ever treated unjustly by the city. I want to get to the bottom of this."

The Mayor's intervention worked almost immediately. Within a few days, he spurred a call to me from the City Attorney and things began to change.

"There is not enough ammunition in the case to warrant a jury. That is the way these cases go most of the time," the City Attorney said easily.

Not what I wanted to hear, but not a surprise either. I was dealing with an attitude that things were predetermined. I had been advised against getting my hopes up by a friend from work who had pursued a domestic violence case herself. She knew the pitfalls and had shared them with me.

"I received your letter explaining what happened. The case will be decided by a judge. We do not have a court advocate," he continued, referring to a question in my letter. "You'll be able to speak that day; it is the victim's right. Prepare something to read to the court."

The judge deciding my case was known in town as a womanizer. I worked with a former flight attendant who knew him and had an affair with him for several years. She did not hold him in high regard. This wasn't good.

Writing the letter was the light I needed to feel hopeful. I began with an outline and wrote diligently every night until our day in court. I almost filled half a legal pad, revising often and reading aloud many times. I read pages and pages from my journal and cried and screamed as I prepared, but I kept going as I transferred much of it to the letter. I knew I was on to something that was good for me.

Despite the Mayor's efforts, no meeting time was set up to prepare anything prior to court. Apparently, ten stitches in the back of my head did not qualify me for a consultation. My whole case was prepared from the police report, the letter I wrote from my journal entries, and the City Attorney's one brief call to me.

The day we met the judge at trial, the City Attorney and I talked a few minutes outside the courthouse. That was it. He was not reassuring or helpful. We walked into the court room barely speaking, almost strangers ready to determine my fate.

MY DAY IN COURT

The crime was not referred to as assault and battery. With this judge it went immediately to a misdemeanor. No jury was called. None of my neighbors who had witnessed what happened were called in to speak. The sympathetic police officer who had investigated the incident and visited me in the emergency room to ask more questions—and had been so kind to me—had moved to Colorado months before we went to court.

The Enemy represented himself, which was his right. He revealed himself to be a fool with his swagger as he entered the courtroom. His ego got the best of him when he attempted to be lawyer-like with his questioning and pacing in the court room as he asked me questions.

He was lost in his own defense while eagerly telling the judge I did not listen to him, and was wrong that night by not allowing him into my home. He could not see his behavior was wrong from the start, typical of many Defendants in these cases.

There was no one there for me except God, but He proved to be enough. Although I was victimized by the court system with an uninterested City Attorney, no jury, no advocate, and no one in the court system willing to get to really know my case, I felt God's grace. In my heart I sensed a small victory coming.

As the victim, I was the state's witness, the state was the Plaintiff. I was not the one who pressed charges, the state did that. Unless the City Attorney was interested enough in my case to ask questions, this meeting with the judge could end in an hour.

As his own lawyer, the Enemy called upon me for questioning, a very awkward and painful situation, considering the City Attorney didn't have any questions for me. Nor did he pose questions to the Enemy. The case was a low priority file as sure as it was anything. Things moved quickly—too quickly. I was getting nervous. My hands were shaking.

"You may now address the court, Miss Brooks," the judge offered.

I read my statement as if it were my last will and testament. The Enemy was not allowed to comment. He asked to do so but was refused. This was empowering. I was not interrupted. I was heard. I said what I needed to say and didn't hold back, my voice rising to a crescendo before I finished.

"You lied to me and used me. You hurt me when I could not defend myself. You left me in a bloody mess. You were not sorry; you were never sorry," I blurted out. "You've lied as long as I've known you. About whom you really are and what you are about. You violated me over and over again and never cared about how much you hurt me," I continued, with quivering hands, but a steady voice. "You left me for dead. I knew you would. It was always about you."

I told the judge about the white fog and the blood and the bruises and how I still could not remember what happened that night to cause the gash to my head that resulted in ten stitches. I went on to talk about the anger in the Enemy's eyes when he broke through the back door, and the vile sounds that came from his mouth that were so frightful. I talked about my post-traumatic stress and what was left for me to endure after two years of fear building inside of me.

All my emotions poured out like water rushing downstream. This was my chance to purge myself of a lot of anger. Despite who was there, I took my chance to spew my anger in a descriptive view from my eyes and not from the police report. I did not stop until I was completely exhausted. The judge did not stop me either.

No Thrill of Victory

With a conviction in hand for just a few short months, and an opportunity for Civil Court, I feared retaliation by the Enemy, but continued to move forward. The City of Scottsdale Court had not shown him they meant business. They did not take my case seriously.

"There will be no jail time or charge of felony assault and battery since this is your first conviction," the judge gifted to him. "I could do both, but I am going to give you an opportunity to turn your life around."

The Enemy was convicted of misdemeanor assault and told to pay a minimal fine of $1,000 to the court. The fine included my court fees, too, but no restitution to me.

"You are also instructed to do anger management classes through the City of Scottsdale; the bailiff will handle that for you later. You must adhere to an Order of Protection issued by the Court," the judge added. "This is a generous offer. I hope you realize this and abide by all of it. I don't want to see you back here again."

The Enemy acknowledged the judge but said nothing. He often lied and could easily convince people he did not fit the crime and made an attempt to do that this time, too. "I have too many personal conflicts to meet the demands of these classes," he told the judge.

The judge did not waiver. The Enemy may not have done the classes. I didn't follow-up.

Despite my intensifying post-traumatic stress, all documented in my letter to the City Attorney, the Enemy walked out of court that day with his own sense of victory. He was given few instructions by the judge. I was naïve to think it would be any other way.

The Enemy left the courtroom that day with his new girlfriend on his arm. He was smug with his head held high. He gave me his smirk, as if he had not really been convicted of anything.

His girlfriend was sheepish with her head bent. I pitied her. I would pray for her. She was about to be a fool. She did not look at me again after I read my letter. My gut told me she had shame she could not identify. She would surely succumb to his brutal behavior; it was hard to avoid. She had been affected by my words, it showed in her stride. Maybe they would linger and she would hear them more clearly another time.

I walked out of the courtroom alone and confidant I had done my part. It was over. I exited from the same parking garage as they did. It was a surreal moment, but not disturbing to me. I had left my anger in the courtroom.

CIVIL COURT DECISION

I frantically worked to convince my attorney friend to take my case and begin the process in Civil Court. He wasn't encouraging, but willing to try. He had represented me in a civil suit with a car accident the year before; I trusted him, he had done a good job in the past. To win real justice would be bittersweet.

"We'll get him where it hurts; in his wallet," my lawyer promised me. "This is going to set a precedent if we win. We're reaching on this one. The case will be labeled domestic violence. Although you never lived together, or had children together, you had a romantic relationship," he stated emphatically.

"You have a documented history with the police, which means you would have had a better chance in court if you had never met this person before that night," he continued. "If he had randomly assaulted you in a public place, it would easily be assault and battery. But you have a two-year personal history; you fall into the domestic violence abyss, the category of misdemeanor assault. That is the law."

"I can't resist the temptation to sue him. There is a chance to make him pay. It's not in my best interest to let it go. I need closure," I persisted. "I have to go forward for me and for the women struggling to break free."

"I insist you use a private investigator," he proceeded, with caution and concern.

I believed in this wholeheartedly. I wasn't trying to coerce him into a poor use of time and energy. I respected his apprehension by letting him call the shots.

THE ENEMY

The Enemy was an arrogant fool, insisting on defending himself again. He was not prepared, showing no notes or research to support his case. He again waltzed in to court as if it was his arena.

The Enemy was out of his league representing himself. He had never gone to law school nor taken any law classes that I knew of; his field was chemistry and research. I doubted he had even a friend or family member in the field of law.

How much time he had spent in a courtroom was not known, but that still would not qualify him to take on these trials. It was obvious my attorney preferred dealing with lawyers who were experienced, so they could work together toward a good resolution. He wanted our day in court to be a quick turn-around.

"I endured the Enemy's questions in criminal court. Will I have to go through that again in Civil Court?" I asked my lawyer.

"This process can't be avoided unless I circumvent some of his questions with objections and counter-questions. But remember, this time you're a survivor and not a victim."

"Yes. It's going be easier this time to stand up for myself and find my power."

PREPARATION

I made notes of what I needed to do to convince the Civil Court judge I was injured both financially and emotionally. I listed all the times I was not able to interview for a career change position after graduate school because post-traumatic stress had overtaken my entire existence and made my life small.

I researched for information on what precedents had been set on cases similar to mine. There were no other cases. I used journal writing to release my emotions, especially my anger, and I prayed a lot for the courage to carry through with my plans.

The euphoria of peace came over me more frequently if I followed this regimen. I was much calmer than I had been in years. I did not overreact as much toward every little thing. Although life seemed like a movie, I sensed the start of a new life. I wrote in my journal each day beginning with a question. It was important to me to understand what was happening. This was somebody else's story, somebody I used to be.

I followed a simple routine of when I went to bed and when I rose in the morning. I stayed on task when I started something and worked on only one thing at a time. I was often numb as a protection mechanism. There was not much forward motion in the sea. The tide almost stood still. I gingerly faced the day stuck in the denial stage of grief for the loss of a life I might never know, but persisted with self-defense towards my wounds. Fear became my motivator. I hung on to my faith and prayed for survival.

A Win is a Win

My win in Civil Court set a precedent by the amount awarded for a domestic violence case. It was an important victory, both in its achievement and in the amount of $12,000 of restitution.

The Phoenix judge did not hesitate to move swiftly and ruled that the restitution be paid promptly and that justice be served. "I have seen too many of these cases go unpunished," he said. "I am willing to help you." It was as if he had been waiting for me and my case.

The court order was ignored by the Enemy. He disappeared within a few weeks. My private investigator made a few attempts to find him, but to no avail. My attorney had few ideas and kept watching for the Enemy to make the first move.

"This is very common," he said. "We should wait it out. We can go back to court at a later date and take another action."

Neither of these ideas made sense or were acceptable to me. I was not going to lose by allowing the Enemy to not be punished. The convictions were not enough. The Enemy needed to be punished and he needed to pay. This much I knew for sure.

TAKING ACTION

"I need to take things into my own hands or I will never see a dime," I told my girlfriend at lunch soon after the civil trial. "I need to know closure."

"You will heal from taking action," she said encouragingly.

I was empowered by her words. During our lunch conversation I found the motivation I needed to investigate the situation on my own. My anger was increasing and to my advantage.

We were in a restaurant just down the street from the dealership where the Enemy had his BMW repaired. The first part of my plan was to chase down the Enemy's personal information through his distinctive foreign sedan.

I walked into that dealership with some confidence and asked the receptionist to help me. Sneaking around was not foreign to me; I had stalked the Enemy almost as much as he had stalked me.

I earned the young woman's trust by passionately telling my story. I was brazen in my efforts but also sincere. Despite my nervousness, I was straight-forward. She sensed truthfulness in the telling. Empathy showed in her wide eyes. Did she have a similar story?

She easily gave me the information I so desperately needed, possibly illegally, but within a few minutes. She found it all on her computer: his new work address and phone number.

"The dealership delivered his serviced car there just a few weeks back. These records are current," she said quietly. "This is what you need. I am pretty sure he is still at this workplace." She slid a piece of paper toward me.

"Thank you, thank you," I said with a grateful smile. Her look of concern told me she was done and I should go. I left quickly.

My next step was to confirm he was at this workplace. The Enemy had changed companies several times since the assault, so I had to be sure. There could be no mistakes. I avoided the receptionist at the ON Gas Company and called the Human Resources office from the lobby phone.

"He is here on contract," the person on the other end of the phone said with no hesitation. "Is there anything else you need?"

"No. Thank you for your help. Thank you very much."

I had what I wanted. I had put myself in a precarious position, but it worked out. "Have I broken the law in any way?" I mumbled to myself as I started the car. "I must act quickly. I have come too far to quit."

If I did not finish the job here and garnish his wages, no one would do it. If he learned of my actions and left town, it would all be over with no restitution. "Please God protect me and help me continue with my plan."

At a convenience store nearby, I phoned my attorney. "He works at the ON Gas Company on McDowell. You need to move fast," I continued breathlessly, "He's on contract. The Human Resources people will confirm all of this."

"Slow down. I need more details," he laughed. "I will get on it today, now go home and wait for me to call." He heard urgency in my voice.

"Is it illegal to do what I did? It feels okay in my heart. All of the pieces fell in place today," I said at a high speed, after laying out the events of the day.

"This is good work; be proud. You got it done."

He moved quickly and the ON Gas Company did, too. The necessary paperwork was setup by the end of the day and the garnishment was issued. The private investigator we hired to help me had no part in the final outcome. He did not contact me to say congratulations. That was not important. We were getting paid and I felt good.

SHOW ME THE MONEY

Within three weeks the Enemy came to my attorney's office and paid the $12,000 due me. He obviously did not want to deal with the garnishment at his office.

"Some of the cash must be from his mother," I said when I got the call. "She must still believe he is innocent. I doubt he has that kind of cash."

"This is unusual. Normally a garnishment runs its course. Be happy; our office is. You have been a big help."

The investigator's charges were paid immediately, as well as my attorney's thirty-three percent. The money was being cut up quickly. My therapist and chiropractor were paid next. I received the last $6,000. The doctor and emergency room bills had been paid by the Enemy in the criminal court, since I had no insurance. This was a good end result.

My need to win, to save face, began to dissipate. I had sucked the last bit of strength out of myself with this second trial. All my efforts had cost me many sleepless nights, but I was a survivor. I would recover now.

POST-TRAUMATIC STRESS

Despite the success in Civil Court, I went backwards with my health issues of stress and fatigue, migraines and other post-traumatic stress symptoms. I became emotionally detached from my life. The trials had been obsessions. They controlled me even though they were a chance to feel empowered. I did not regret my actions to testify and to sue, but as the weeks went by after the trials, I often found myself staring into the dark night when home alone.

I searched for answers in my prayers to give this entire ordeal a purpose and asked for God's will, hoping that His will was complete closure. My goal to thrive went out of sight at times and I became consumed with grief for my lost innocence. I read more and more about grief, even though I knew the process and had read about it before. On occasion, my AA recovery lost priority and isolation set in. I did not resort to alcohol, but I did turn to hiding out in the darkness of my world.

Is judgment by a few women friends a total lack of support for me? Will I reach out and not let my mind play games with me? Have I hurt myself but not seen it?

Rather than ask for specific help from my sponsor, I settled for the occasional lunch date or phone call with her. By seeking therapy once a week and attending church on occasion, my priest was sometimes my only contact over a weekend. My isolation engulfed me at times and fear crept into my life.

Does anyone have any idea what it is like to be a victim of violent crime with the force of post-traumatic stress on your heels?

I was a tidal wave running a race to an unreachable shore. My body ached and my mind pushed and pulled like the ebb and flow of the tide. Post-traumatic stress was turmoil and chaos. I had been here before. At the beginning of my AA recovery, I had fear and now that fear was back with a vengeance.

"Something needs to be done immediately," I frantically told my therapist. "I have stepped into a hole. I want to get well and start living."

"Psychological trauma is an affliction of powerlessness. The victim is rendered helpless by an overwhelming force. The victim loses control, loses their sense of connection and meaning," she explained. "That is what is happening to you. This is the aftermath of your trauma."

This reaction was overwhelming for me. I was now thrust into a world that was foreign and terrifying. My mere existence was threatened by post-traumatic stress. I was defenseless and vulnerable.

As the weeks went on, I felt the intensity of the stress at a level I had never experienced before. I had suppressed it during those many months leading up and through the trials, a time too difficult to deal with the memories. Anger and fear and grief, and the storm of post-traumatic stress were now my new story.

Just as the weakened sailor alone at sea does not comprehend a successful rescue, I too was discouraged. "How come I struggle to do this again? How do I get out of this vicious cycle and stay out?" I asked my therapist.

"Life is different now," she said calmly. "The terror that remains has disconnected you from yourself, but not forever. We'll find a safer place and a way out."

FORGIVENESS

God, I played a part in this abusive relationship. I could have changed some things. I am a survivor and know that this crazy life can end here. Thank you, God, for watching over me, I know the rest will take time. Some of it is up to me, and the rest I give to you, God.

I began to forgive myself and transform from victim to survivor. The gift to thrive was mine. I had a victory in criminal court, even if small. I saw possibilities of a new life. My heart was lighter. I had gone on to a successful civil trial.

The good news was, I could now truly move on. I didn't need to follow-up on whether he paid the court's fine in Scottsdale. I had no need to make contact again with the City Attorney or the judge at Scottsdale City Court. The Order of Protection was in place.

The restitution was paid. I was done with lawyers for the first time in over a year. God was working in my life as my days were brighter. The wheels of justice had turned slowly, but we were done with God's plan for our lives together. Our relationship had finally ended and I knew it deep in my soul as I said, "I forgive you and I forgive me."

Spiritual Transformation

We are not human beings having a spiritual experience.
We are spiritual beings having a human experience.
Teilhard de Charden

The Challenge

At the end of my time with the Enemy, my world was very small. I had almost forgotten what the sunshine felt like on my skin or how the sound of rain could renew my soul. The things I thought were normal were bizarre. I lived in a secret world that I told no one about for fear of ridicule.

My challenge was to make things right when they could barely be charted on an even course. My spiritual state was comatose, lost at sea. Tossed by the waves of his cruelty, the Enemy's coercive control dominated my thoughts.

The answer was, and had always been, to go forward with God and sail full speed against high swells. Many months of therapy and group sessions had enlightened me again to prayer. I no longer bought the shame of the Enemy's vindictive words. His hurtful ways of treating me like I was less than he was were removed from my psyche as I listened to God's messages in my recovery meetings. Daily positive affirmations filled my thoughts.

I had been down a dark path of self-destruction with the Enemy, but it was a learning experience, too. He had brainwashed me. Things were messy and uncomfortable, and letting go of my guilt was a step to spiritual growth.

I did not regret my past, but challenged it in my writing. I learned a lot about the coercive control he practiced by talking through those two years in therapy. I dealt with the complexity of the post-traumatic stress symptoms first. I was always on high alert. Fearfulness at every turn needed to be addressed so I could function. I lived in the moment and worked at feeling secure and getting my life back to a safe place.

"You did not deserve to be assaulted, anytime, anywhere. You trusted the wrong person for too long," my therapist reassured me early on. "You did not know when to walk away and admit it was an abusive situation."

"I know," I said in agreement. "I stayed to try to fix it, fighting for a chance to make all the wrong things right. It was almost intolerable, but now I own what was mine.

The challenge was to find recovery for my post-traumatic stress symptoms and recognize my spiritual strengths. I saw myself as a whole person standing tall and emotionally secure. But there was no guarantee. I just had to believe it.

These were uncharted waters for me as I surveyed the wreckage of a lifetime of low self-esteem. This was a growth opportunity on my spiritual journey. It seemed daunting, but a welcomed challenge. Was it possible? Would I find balance?

THE AWAKENING

This abusive relationship I had endured was not over when the violence stopped. There were hindrances that had an impact on my spirituality. The lack of jail time for the Enemy after the criminal trial tested my faith in our judicial system. I was afraid of what would happen if I needed protection from him in the future.

My struggles to trust and to pray with conviction were very real. I had a hard time focusing on God and had to concentrate intensely to get to a quiet place. The chaos in my soul calmed and I found answers after long times spent in prayer. I used my meditation time to guide my thoughts and prayers, practicing quietly each morning.

My spiritual life had been stagnant, despite my going to church and attending my Alcoholic Anonymous meetings. I was often in the wrong place at the wrong time, asking "Where is God?" My new recovery began when I accepted difficult realities about myself. I took a hard look at my brokenness from love addiction.

There were other unhealthy relationships along the way. I flirted with the devil out of loneliness. Fear sabotaged my spiritual growth. I could not predict how God would work in my heart but I trusted my instinct.

My recovery from trauma was long and arduous. My spiritual strength came back to me as time accumulated into a new life of hope. I talked to God in the morning and then reflected on Him in my journal. I thanked God at night for my day. He did not give me more than I could handle.

I am in gratitude and acceptance. I have recovered physically. The bruises have gone away. The gash in my head is healed and my hair has grown back. My power has returned with this connection to God. I have transformed myself one day at a time. God, show me what to do, what to focus on next. The time to share my joy is now; give me guidance.

It was time to connect to myself and also to others. I collected all my driftwood sent in with the tide. I valued only a few pieces that were right for me. The beauty was in the uniqueness of the piece. Just like whom I was as a woman, the beauty was within the weathered wood.

To capture the spirit and quality of the life I longed for, I chose *me* for the first time in my life. I no longer bowed to the Enemy's mind games, unwarranted jealousy and rage. I satisfied my spiritual hunger by turning to God. I did not make quick decisions about anything without prayer. I listened intently instead of acting in haste.

With my eyes wide open, my heart was full of grace. Why had I thought I was different? Like the many pebbles on the beach, I was just like other abused women.

MY PURPOSE

My spiritual transformation was beautiful. God determined the time for my awakening. My spiritual journey had brought me to a place like a vision of home, of the slow sunrise at the horizon of Lake Michigan when dew rests everywhere. God revealed to me what I needed to learn.

I had been thrown out of a car one night, and beaten in a parking garage. These were serious lessons learned for a reason. It was not for me to ask God why, or to question my purpose. I pondered what had happened to me and what I had learned, and was still for God's answers.

What will I do with my life? Will I be happy? Will I make a difference in the world?

On a spiritual quest for many years, I now saw a transformation I had only vaguely believed possible. Hope filled my daily meditation. With will and determination, true spirituality was being achieved. Hope was my driving force.

In search of the rare pieces of me lost at sea, a flood of tears and a tidal wave of emotion emerged as I spent time alone in prayer. I had not cried like that in years. I was so shut down I thought I had forgotten how to cry. An inner strength, unique and significant to my soul, showed itself like flowers protruding through the final snow of spring. I embarked on a journey of wonder, realizing that I had the will to thrive.

I exposed myself and "got naked" emotionally with brutal honesty. It was with my faith that I did not conceal anything about the abuse and violence when telling my stories. I was in pursuit to get to the heart of me. I explored all I had been through.

"I will not compare myself to those who cohabitated, or were married and had children with their abuser. They were not me," I proudly told my therapist. "I will not dumb down my story even though it does not fit the stereotype. My trust in God tells me I have a story, too."

This is more than a mid-life crisis. This is a rebirth for me. I am becoming a new person, the person I always knew I could be. I will not miss this precious time to verbalize my thoughts to God or sweep away the debris of life strewn at my feet.

In meditation, I became aware that having been disenchanted with my situation was a blessing. It motivated me to go further in my spiritual quest. I was desperate, yet hopeful. My transformation had come alive since I faced Death's door. My spirituality grew as I lay in the emergency room waiting to be stitched up. It was my time for grace and healing, an opportunity to take my spiritual life to a new level without ridicule of my relationship with God.

My spiritual transformation included morning quiet time to listen for God's word. It was a slow and tedious process, but it was a start. I did not dismiss what I heard. I took a harder look at what I had to do. Just like climbing the sand dunes above Lake Michigan for the first time in early summer, there was exaltation. My heart soared with that same wonder. I was as alive as I had ever been. I heard God's message to forget negativity. This was a new beginning, a renewal of my identity. I envisioned a better life, calmer seas, someone to love, someone to love me.

EMOTIONAL MATURITY

My emotional maturity traveled far from waiting for the Enemy to return to me. He had often put me in second place but now my needs came first. My boundaries expanded like the blue of the Lakes past the breakwater. My mental restrictions fell away. My new consciousness emerged. It was exhilarating to travel in this light. My spiritual quest was a sincere commitment to my faith.

I yearn for peace and quiet. God, help me to find spiritual truths and to understand my inner mysteries. What spiritual growth plan should I develop?

SACRED CONCERN

My ten-plus years and my Alcoholics Anonymous 12-Step Recovery took me to God for answers. I was comfortable pursuing my new recovery from a spiritual angle. I had been there before. Divine Will worked for me. The Catholic Church was part of my spiritual base. The traditional teachings were not enough, and sometimes too much. A simple path to know a healing God that I could talk to and write to when I needed Him was critical to my recovery.

I released the burdens of shame by praying desperately for help. I had a deep trust in God, and a sacred concern for women like me who suffered from abuse. My feelings of abandonment had haunted me. I saw how I was needy, almost desperate.

I had not known when to leave the Enemy or how to differentiate coercive control from love. I had no role model. *Guide me, God. I am up to the challenges of a full recovery. I have hope.*

TRANSFORMING

My pain flowed in and out. My emotional wounds scarred deeply. My love obsession bound me like a barnacle to wet rocks. As these wounds healed, I anticipated a full recovery. The physical hurt did not go to my soul. It took time to transform and find a place of peace. God eventually reconnected me with the world I had disconnected from when the Enemy kept me from seeing my friends.

My new routine was different, simpler. My language was not even remotely the same. The fear-based way I expressed myself during the two years I was captive with the Enemy had dissipated. My tone was more serene. It was comfortable to be spiritually transforming. I sensed movement to a higher plateau, and knew that I would flourish.

I no longer saw myself as a victim, a role that was not even an option for me anymore. It served no purpose. Now I strolled down the street with my head held high. I was a survivor.

No longer needing to choose risky behavior to appease the Enemy and keep the peace, I sought enrichment. I chose quiet time. Just as the beach line on Lake Michigan changes every summer with the tide, my life changed, too. It was in God's hands.

A clear vision of what my life should be revealed itself to me. What was right and possible for my future transpired as I opened up my heart. I instinctively knew the answers to things I had to decide. God showed me that there are two ways of knowing—one with prayer and writing to look for answers, and one with quiet time to wait and listen.

"The psychological torment of the lies and deception to control you, and the living in fear you knew too well, are all erased," my therapist encouraged me.

"I surrendered to this path," I said. "I know there is peace for me as a survivor, and even more so as a 'sister' of those in the abused women's group. I will continue to travel down the road of recovery, be open and put myself in a good place."

SERVING OTHERS

I listened intently to the other women's stories in our group sessions, ever mindful of how fortunate I was not to be physically scarred. I had empathy for my group. The assault was a tipping point for me. My presence in the group was helpful to others. I allowed the miracle to happen. I did not judge the ones who still lived with their abusers. I did not shun the ones who still wanted to work out their relationships and kept making excuses.

I accept the challenges of my new beginning. God, keep fear from shutting me out of a good life. Thank you God, but for your grace, that is not me telling lies.

Even though their tales of woe were often much different than mine, our stories were the same in many ways. We had all lost ourselves in the life and control of our abuser. Most of us had another aspect to our life that did not coincide with the life of abuse. We were almost two different people trying to live a normal life while being stuck in the chaos. Almost all of us could not see the muck and mire until we were at Death's door.

My spiritual growth moved forward when I recognized myself in all of them. I saw their faces as mine when they shared their stories. They gave me another awareness of abuse that I did not experience, but needed to hear.

I was genuinely grateful for them. I loved them all equally, and asked God daily for a way to serve them. I attended the sessions and listened carefully. I did not think about myself during those times. Sharing space with these like-minded women gave me power. Each of us served the group in our own way. We honored the universal truth that women are the same all over the world. Their hearts and souls, loves and fears resembled mine. I was no longer a chaotic shipwreck. I had a soul-infused personality that merged with my spiritual life.

With all of this new awareness, I acknowledged my two great needs—sharing and solitude. I continued to explore them. We were sisters in our struggles and triumphs. Our camaraderie was significant. I strengthened my understanding of my faith in solitude by getting closer to nature in early morning hikes up Camelback Mountain to find my center with the sunrise. I awakened to my true self, breaking the shell that once hid the real me.

Satisfying My Soul Hunger

I was no longer cynical or skeptical. I kept an open mind to all God had in store for me. My life was heading down a long road of exploration. I satisfied my soul's hunger with positive self-talk while writing affirmations in my journal.

Forgiveness of myself and others arrived as the anger dissipated. The abuse I had lived with for so long shaped my life with narrow thinking. Now I spent time with only those who could help me find my capacity to love. My spiritual path took me there.

A friend in my AA home group became my most unlikely comrade. We began to open up to each other. She had suffered abuse, too, and reached out to me after hearing me share a small part of my story. Most of our life stories varied, but this part on abuse did not. We knew control; we knew loneliness and we knew shame.

My objective was to listen to anything that could possibly help me heal. I morphed into the newly free butterfly. The caterpillar was no more, once the cocoon opened. I let go of the outer layers I had piled on for so long to protect me from the Enemy and his abuse. I visualized them fading away. I witnessed change in me with more confidence and a gentler approach to life.

I was receptive to healing experiences like a baby duckling venturing into the lake for the first time. The search for inner integrity was part of my spiritual quest. This was an opportunity to listen to my soul's hunger and be open to God's definition of myself.

My prayers were full of my hope. I shared my thoughts more freely with women in recovery. God's angels called me to hear the vibrations of my soul. I was not sure how far I would go, but I implemented this awareness into my journal each morning.

Who am I and how strong can I really be? I can be tested and taken further. I am transforming the deepest aspects of my spirit. I will never be the same again. What will be the shape of my life going forward?

PURIFYING MYSELF

It was not easy to release my old familiar habits. They were comfortable and hard to let go of, although they hurt me. They worked in their own odd ways. To face them, I cleansed myself by letting go of needing people, to avoid bringing the wrong people into my life.

I changed where I went and what I did in almost all areas of my life. Making better choices about how I spent my time and who I was with was paramount to my success. I was stretched but my endurance seemed limitless. I did away with people who did not support me in order to evolve spiritually and shape my capacity to love. I settled in for the long haul. I blossomed and survived.

My newer friendships are like tattered sneakers from a past summer. My new persona fits me, too. I accept the changes. I am making peace with the sea and all its creatures to stay afloat to live my faith.

AWAKENING TO MY TRUE SELF

I accepted my responsibility to break the chain of events that had caused me so much harm. Like the sandbags on the beach, I stopped the rushing water from coming closer. I was in control now in most facets of my life. I was free to make choices and to be myself. My true self began to appear.

I removed the fear that had gripped me for so long by gingerly venturing outdoors on warm spring nights, and going to places that I once feared. I counted my blessings. I prayed for hope that post-traumatic stress would not be ever-present. I learned as much about it as I could, talking to professionals who could help me.

With a chance now to expand my life, I took the risk of moving back to my old neighborhood where the assault took place. With reasonable precautions, such as alerting someone that I would be attending an event and to look for me, or making sure I was not out after dark, I accepted social invitations that were enjoyable: movies, coffee shops and small restaurants. I worked to come alive by being cognizant of my actions. I owed myself this freedom and appreciated all I was given. I did not dwell on what had been taken away.

My faith told me that my history would not repeat itself. I spoke out to make it better for the women seeking help and I found sheer joy in doing so. I was not just a survivor of another crime of passion. I was a comrade for other women who trudged down this path.

Women who had come through the other end with grace and dignity were my strength. I stood with them to find the shoreline. To declare, "I walk in their shoes" meant removing the clutter from my path. Sharing my story and helping other women was the pinnacle of my spiritual transformation. Moving through life with God's grace was an added blessing. I was awakening to my true self.

Dear Nicole

Love gives itself, and is not bought.
Henry Wadsworth Longfellow

Sisters

The Nicole Brown Simpson tragedy occurred six months after I was assaulted. It could have been deadly for me, too. Watching her story unfold on TV was mesmerizing. I identified with her, but the comparisons I should have made early did not happen. I recognized OJ's mask and fury. I knew it well. I saw her as "different" from me in many ways and stood my ground on having a unique experience.

They were celebrities. They had been married and had children. All the justifications were there to tell you my story was unlike hers. Not only was it difficult to see my emotional connection to her, but I was not willing to face her tragedy.

It was purely entertainment until I started writing to her in my journal in preparation for going to trial. Then her story became a crashing ship against rocks in a storm.

Dear Nicole,

Will he get away with it? Will anyone else be pursued for your murder? My anger is surfacing in conversations about celebrities, blacks and blondes and high-powered lawyers. I am in the throes of understanding my own domestic violence, but I am your soul sister.

I, too, have been abused many times, minimizing the situation and going back again and again. This will not happen to me, Nicole. I am not you. I am smarter. How did your family and friends let this happen to you? You had three sisters. Did they not care about you?

Having been obsessed with an attractive African American male myself, I believed I had the hook, but actually it was the line and sinker. What at first was the anchor, became the dead weight of drowning.

I was tied to Nicole, defending her actions as I learned more about her. I fell back into my insanity easily. Not seeing that for a long time only added to my part in her drama. Knowing that was painful. Nicole had done the same. To know it about her was even more painful.

MANIPULATION

Usually seen by others as being independent, I did a good job portraying what I wanted them to see. At the expense of losing my soul, I became what The Enemy wanted. I aimed to please. Nicole was quoted once saying she was sculpted by OJ. I shuddered when I read it.

The control and abuse had been ugly. The coercive control had manifested as post-traumatic stress. The OJ trial began. I learned Nicole had a rebellious side, just as I did. After reading many of the articles written about her, I wondered if that had added to her chaotic life.

Physical pain showed first in migraine headaches as I became addicted to her story. At times, I had no energy to do anything else. Fear lingered. I realized some of my poor health was caused by my attitude. As the lone survivor at sea for days, I could easily succumb to the call of the deep, no longer hanging on.

Dear Nicole,

Your murder is getting real to me. It is frightening. I feel it physically, with tightness in my chest, an ache in my stomach. How did this happen to you? How did you find yourself in the wrong place? Was there no protection for you? Is there no protection for me? I am shocked by your life. I have come to see the world through the Enemy's eyes. Did you do that, too? I am afraid of what I see, Nicole, in your story portrayed on TV. It is not me, or is it? I have to watch, as if to be there for you.

ESCAPING

Nicole appeared to not know how to get to where she really wanted to be—secure and happy—and neither did I. Her abuser was relentless when she tried to find that place, and so was mine. Obsessions mounted to an insane crescendo. We were powerless. I, too, was brain-washed as sure as if I had been lured into a fanatical cult. It would be a long way back. Time had stopped for me; my world was small.

Dear Nicole,

I know you. We want to be the people we know inside ourselves, the ones that ache to find our souls. Did you lack the will to do anything about it, Nicole, as if it did not matter anymore? Did you know what was coming down the road for you? Did you numb yourself with other men to ease the pain as I did? Did you lose hope that you deserved more? Did you cling to a sinking lifeboat?

I am so frustrated. The newspaper headlines glare with your brutal murder. I neglect myself. I forget to eat or sleep. I obsess on the terror. Did you do that, too? Yes you did; we're sisters, and you're tied to me.

The irony was that I went to work each day with a great group of people who respected me. I told no one. I was on the edge, living vicariously through Nicole's life. She told no one for years either. I understood.

I left the TV off at night, abandoning Nicole in some way, fooling only a few people that things were grand. I continued this charade to escape for most of that year. Terror resonated in my brain. I would try to take control, but fear would consume me just as if a tidal wave was washing over the beach during a storm.

The stress seemed endless. It was circling and it was not going to change for me, no matter what I did, until I was willing to surrender to God and ask for help. Fear had been forced on me like the threat of mutiny aboard ship. Facing Death's door was now real to me. In her last days, Nicole knew that, too.

PANIC

When too many panic attacks had my attention, I attempted to take stock of myself. I was numb, which is almost as bad as suicidal. It is the step before no longer wanting life. Nicole had been there.

My friends were busy with their lives. They did not know my panic. I hid out in my craziness, my small chaotic world. Nobody noticed. I lived in a vacuum. The wear-and-tear on my body, my psyche and my soul resembled wearing down rocks on the shore. It was a battle at sea, with rage that put me in danger very easily.

Dear Nicole,

You had that rage, too. You did not want rules laid down, conditions set, as you began to find yourself. It was all over your stressful face in the pictures revealed by the media. You knew panic. You were never offered a compromise were you?

Behind your beautiful smile was the face of domestic violence. It takes one to know one, and I know you. Judging by your risky behavior, you had almost given up.

I often do not know what to do with my sadness. Escaping into my loneliness in the panic zone is a new kind of terror. It is what I do now, even though the violence has stopped.

ADDICTED

Being addicted to chaos was what I had known. There was no quick release. The fighting had been futile. Relentless arguments Nicole knew, too. It had been war for us with no one declaring a truce, pathetic situations.

My body would react as if I had been in a fight. I searched a long time for God in the depths of my soul. I became non-existent, similar to the shell behind Nicole's smile. The horizon disappeared for us as we sailed off course.

The Enemy had brainwashed me, but now I was at a turning point in my life. I needed him to not be an obsession far beyond my control.

Dear Nicole,

Did you know that wave? I think you did. You were tied down by intimidation, too. Did you ask for more out of life? I hope so. You were more than just a pretty face. You understood this. Life was constantly in an upheaval for you, too. The simplest things escaped us. We lived under the radar of the real world.

It appeared you had so much going for you and that you would walk away, but you could not. I get that. I know what it is like to want to try one more time, to not be sure and to make the same mistakes over and over.

Patricia L. Brooks

BLINDSIDED

Because of my shame, I never investigated the things he told me about himself. By not pushing to meet his friends and family, I told myself it did not matter and I made myself less important to him. My low self-esteem took over. Meeting anyone in his life only happened by coincidence or careful planning, and only in the rarest of situations.

He had always aggressively pursued me. I bought into being wrong to question anything he said. If I did not trust him and do what he wanted, he raged. He had me with shame and used it against me. I saw that in the OJ trial testimonies, too. My unhappy life was thrust at me again, like the bow of a threatening ship in a sea battle.

Dear Nicole,

You knew this trick. You were conned into telling far more than you should have ever confided. While sleeping with the Enemy, our trust was used against us. We formed a highly volatile bond with them. Comparing us to others and questioning our every move was a cruel way to control us, but it was done. You lived what I lived—it is the way of domestic violence.

The Enemy twists much of what I say to make me feel less than. I know you knew this place. It has been shown to me in your story.

God sends out alerts. I rarely heed the warning signs. I keep coming back to my lonely self. I see you have done this, too. Sleep peacefully. Your struggle is over.

160

PASSIONATE

The Enemy and I had a passionate relationship built around his goal of controlling me and my fear of making mistakes. It worked. The knot he tied around my neck did not shut off my anger. It hit my hot button.

The emotional abuse was worse than the physical abuse. It was much harder to overcome the cruel words and mind games. They were subtle and cunning and stirred the post-traumatic stress in me. They lingered indefinitely.

Although passionate about my personal and business goals, I was incapable of being whole and a fully functioning person. All my positive energy went to teaching at the community college. Everything else seemed to suffer. I had longed to find a way out of that hole, that tunnel to disaster. It was dark and frightening.

Dear Nicole,

There has to be a light out there but where is it? Watching your murder trial gives no answers. It often seemed senseless, just for show, but I believe, Nicole, you were a passionate person fighting to be your own person, too.

Why can't I find God? Why do I feel my faith is lost?

Nicole, were you depressed or scared out there on your own? Did you suffer anxiety attacks like I do, and feel helpless? Did you have debilitating bouts with fear and stress? Were you floundering in the water, too?

161

BETRAYAL

The betrayal for me was the violation of my own moral principles. We sold our souls, Nicole and me. We betrayed ourselves and each other.

Those last months of my involvement with the Enemy got down to my not even caring that other women were in the picture. Nicole lived that life. Her friends told the media repeatedly of psychological abuse from his constant infidelity and attitude of entitlement.

If The Enemy called or did not call, if he showed up at midnight or not for a week, it did not matter. I had succumbed to a life of nonresistance. Nicole knew this life. We had decided that if it was "only" verbal abuse, it was a major improvement.

Beaten and tired when I heard her story, I was frozen in time. Waiting for him to not stalk me or pursue me anymore, I prayed he would see me as dead prey. But like OJ, he could not let me go, even if he didn't want me anymore. He would shun me and then show me off. OJ was described as doing the same thing.

Just as the tides during early spring are consistent, each day was the same. I had no strength of mind or body. My life stood still. My lighthouse was not vibrant. Nicole had lost her glow, too, long before that knife crossed her throat.

I would humiliate myself after a long argument and go weak in the heart and dead in my soul. He could not stop manipulating me. I could not stop betraying myself until I faced Death's door.

Nicole and OJ had been on that treadmill, too. And now he was at her funeral.

The Enemy often forced me to open my door, to let him into my bed. My world was a ship disappearing over the horizon. I hated him for it, but could not stop doing what I had done for so long. I was addicted, as sure as if I was shooting him into my arm.

Dear Nicole,

I am pitiful and trapped, crying out for help. I yell to the wind on an imaginary beach because that is what we women in violence do. Nicole, do you yell at the ocean? I am sure of it. I can see you in my mind's eye.

I know you felt that helplessness, too. You had that need to change things, that passion for a connection, that addiction to the fantasy of love. I get you. I pray for you. Rest in peace, dear one. I will live for both of us.

ISOLATION

With each day looming like a dark cloud on Lake Michigan, I isolated myself from the world and submerged myself in sadness. My tortured self knew things had been dire. Nicole knew her demise was imminent. What was in store for me?

I was alone with my thoughts and fears, as if lost on an island, with no place to put my heartache. Post-traumatic stress stole many parts of me. I became sludge on the beach after a storm. I did not see myself deserving a better life. All my hopes and dreams had diminished to a diploma in a folder at the bottom of my closet, alongside a box with the cap and gown I had laid to rest. Forgetting they were there, I lost sight of my life.

Even with therapy and group sessions, there was a missing link in me. I was stuck in the grip of post-traumatic stress. Blind to so much, the weight of my stress hovered over me. I still could not see my losses as gifts and be grateful.

I had so much energy when I met the Enemy, so much drive, so much confidence. When did my personality erode to a woman in fear, hiding from life?

Dear Nicole,

Were you screaming to get out as I was, but stuck in the darkness? Were you pushed into the tunnel of doom? Did OJ's abuse carve away at the vibrant, positive and upbeat person you had been? I know that can happen; I just don't know how.

Did you isolate behind your beauty, your children, your party life with your friends? I think of you often, Nicole, not being able to flourish in that stifling marriage. When did you move on? Or did you? Could you?

ANXIETY

Constantly agitated, I had no patience. My time was limited for personal care. My work commitments or my classes took precedence. I lived vicariously through others. I settled for less and was too insecure and anxious to go after more. I was capable of more but could not move in that direction.

My hypertension was reflected in all areas of my life. Common things, such as doors slamming or car tires screeching, upset me. I overreacted often with the OJ trial. I would have a hard time sleeping if I watched a news update of the case.

If someone stood too close behind me, I would ask them to step back. My anxiety was overwhelming. Fear of being attacked was ever-present. Nightmares ran through my mind most nights.

The OJ case was on the news all day and as stressful as it was, I could not stop watching. I prayed for Nicole and her family, and that justice would prevail. It was a constant reminder of what could have been my story.

With a therapist who understood and respected post-traumatic stress, I began the slow journey of recovery. I gave thanks daily, accepting this was part of my journey. I peeled away the onion. Nicole had done that, too, it was well documented in her sisters' words in the trials. She had attempted a new life. I was sure now I could do that, too.

Dear Nicole,

God is not going to give me more than I can handle. Post-traumatic stress has knocked at my door and found its way inside. Did it find you? Were you on high alert, too? I think so. We were often teased by death, weren't we?

Nicole, you're in my heart. We are sisters. This is your story, too. I pray, Nicole, you had support groups and good therapy, and that you did not go it alone. My recovery journey is yours, too. I will not forget you; I will think of you often and remember you when I remember me.

HOOKED

Being hooked on chaos, my head whirled, my heart beat heavily. The circling sharks didn't stop, but encouraged the thumping in my head. I had to find a way to break that vicious cycle. I began to take notice of the people around me. What were their intentions? Should they be in my life? This self-protection worked in my favor, made me stronger. But the real healing began when I attended groups that first focused on domestic violence with work on post-traumatic stress.

At first I felt helpless; all I could do was lash out at the violence I had endured and heard described in Nicole's trial. She was me. A terrible realization came to me as I watched her horror unfold. I had begged for my life more than once, Nicole had many times, too. Our domestic violence was bigger than anyone knew. Her death could surely have been my demise, too.

Dear Nicole,

Did anybody care? My friends and family thought they cared, but usually told me I was strong and to "just call 911." With too many beatings to count, Nicole, you must have heard those words as well.

Your family loves OJ. We all know this from the media stories and from their comments. OJ does a lot for all of them. Did they choose to be blind? God help them if they did. My Enemy's friends were blind, his mother was blind, and I had no one, either.

God has lifted me. Did you seek God Nicole? Did you have faith? Did you start your day with prayers? I pray you had faith. I pray you lost some of your fear of abuse. I pray you withdrew from him so you could get tough.

LOSSES

The greatest loss during this time was the weakening of my faith. Having prided myself on being a faith-based person, a person who believed in God, a spiritual person who had hope, I was often lost in fear and sadness. I had sadness that the Enemy never apologized to me in court, never asked for forgiveness or acknowledged he had done anything wrong. Even after two losses at trial, he never admitted to anything or acknowledged what he took from me. He was always the victim. OJ did the same thing. It was always about him and never his fault.

My weak faith exacerbated my post-traumatic stress, allowing for more suffering. I had a hopeless feeling of doom and despair. I was on a ship sinking into dark, cold waters. No lighthouse blinked, no foghorn called.

Hoping for a fresh start to my faith, I started attending Mass near my home in Scottsdale at the Franciscan Renewal Center. I sought God and prayed for me and others like me, and for Nicole's soul. I found myself on the edge of the crowd, the onlooker at the beach, afraid to venture toward others on the shore.

The migraines, the chest pains, the vertigo, and the numbness in my hands, along with the insomnia, stole my peace. Seeing a chiropractor for the first year was part of the doctor's plan for my damaged neck. The headaches came on a regular basis. Often I went to bed for a day due to the pain. I lost my routine, my life.

The Enemy did not love me. OJ did not love Nicole. We were obsessions for them. They promised monogamy, but never delivered. We knew they were going to hurt us. We lost a lot before the last blow; so much of ourselves wasted on them. They had an image problem and what others thought of them was paramount in their lives. Maybe it was everything.

When I tried to tell a friend about it, she didn't believe me. She said my reality was different from hers. She was not willing to validate me. Nicole had a special friend. I heard about her during the trial and I envied their relationship. My friend could not listen to me, nor be empathetic. She was not really my friend.

Dear Nicole,

When did we stop taking care of ourselves, Nicole? Were we in so much denial about our victimization that we kept repeating that same insane behavior? Did we leave any room for God?

Why did we allow our abusers to turn the blame around and condemn us for getting angry when they bypassed the issue of infidelity? How did we lose our respect—our dignity? If I complained about other women, I was in fear of his wrath. Nicole, I know you lived this, I read about it so often, my heart aches for you.

GOD

Writing through my anger in my journal was my gift to myself, and a gift from God. It helped me heal. I wrote about what it meant to be captured and threatened, to not be respected. I forgave myself for accepting the Enemy's gifts and flowers when I knew it was wrong. I was kind to myself with affirmations I wrote when I did not fully understand what was going on in my head. I wrote for Nicole, too, because her journal had stopped beating.

This process was God's plan to help me rise above the post-traumatic stress. With this freeing activity and God's grace, I knew I would not isolate again; I had some way and someone to take away the pain.

Dear Nicole,

My drug of choice was what you knew, too, Nicole; and the stress associated with it was horrendous, but now I have found another way. I pray you did, too.

My prayer is to live the rest of my life on the inside looking out. I pray for God's help in this. You are in my heart, Nicole. My post-traumatic stress is quicksand that can take me down, but I keep your smile in front of me. You did not die in vain. You were not sacrificed.

My mind no longer plays games. Therapy helps me with the voices still living in my head. God eases my gnawing fears. No longer are there days without smiles. I have broken the cycle for us, Nicole. I am no longer a link in that chain of no phone calls, no contacts, no nothing and no God. Like the anchor caught in the sand at the bottom of the sea, I have pulled long and tugged hard and broken free for both of us. I will not forget you or stop talking about you.

TAKE MY CAR

Life is either a daring adventure or nothing at all.
Security is mostly a superstition. It does not exist in nature.

Helen Keller

SURPRISE

His long serrated knife was too close to my kidneys for me to scream for help. The flash of it at my side froze me in my spot as it reflected off the setting sun. He pinned me to the car door with the blade on the pager at my waist. I stood as still as one of the mannequins in the store window in front of me. His stale breath stained my cheek in the cool air as he stood beside me, too close to me for my taste. His eyes glazed over as he stared me down.

"Where's your purse? he demanded.

"There, back on the trunk," I said, as I pointed to the rear of the car. I had placed it there to retrieve something in the car. A mistake that later became so obvious to me.

A young woman was standing behind him. I froze, and gave her only a glance. No sound, just thinking, *if he wants the purse I'll give it to him.* I feared the knife could slip at any moment

171

and puncture my clothes, or worse. The lowering sun increased my fear like a dark shadow coming over me.

"Where are your keys?" He uttered another demand.

"Here," I said with a shaking hand and no hesitation. I easily gave up my car.

With no other words, he turned around and handed his accomplice my purse and nabbed the keys from me, barely brushing my hand. His hand felt dirty and dry, like his face, weathered from street life. *He must have done this before.* It came so easily to him.

The young woman hovering over his shoulder peered into my purse like a starving animal. She was petite and seemed not to be as street-worn or experienced at this game, but more like a lost soul. Her sad eyes showed me. He quickly removed the knife from my side and jumped into the driver's seat. He commanded her to get in the car, as if she was a nuisance, a tag-along, an after-thought. They sped off before she could even shut her door.

Before I could react, they were off, through the crowd of shoppers who were oblivious to this incident in the beautiful Arizona sunset, strolling with their holiday shopping, chatting and laughing. They never looked beyond their fun, or up from their car trunks as they placed beautiful packages inside.

I watched my car race down 24th Street, run the red light on Camelback Road and fade out of my sight. I could have been kidnapped and pushed into that car to fight for my life, but instead I was running to the Broadway store.

The shock of it gave me cold hands and a wildly beating heart as I bolted into the store. I saw startled expressions on customers as I frantically asked for a phone and a manager. A clerk whisked me to the nearby jewelry department and offered some help. A manager soon appeared, but was more concerned with not making a scene in the store than with my despair. He began nervously assuring people everything was okay. I was directed to a phone stored behind the counter and asked to make the call quietly.

"911. What is your emergency?"

"My car has been stolen. I am at the Biltmore Fashion Park, at the Broadway store. They are heading down 24th Street, speeding in my brown Honda Accord."

"Have you been hurt? Do you need an ambulance?"

"No. Just help me find my car. They have my purse, money and credit cards, too."

"Do not leave the store; the police are on their way."

HELP

As if frozen in time, I stayed there by the jewelry department for about ten minutes. The dispatcher kept me on the phone until a policewoman and a male detective arrived just moments later.

"What kind of car is it?"

"A 1985 Honda Accord; the most stolen car in America," I quipped, trying to relax.

The officer took down a better description of the car and made no comment. She was all business. This was serious and I knew it. It was just hard to face it.

I moved quickly to the outside of the store as the police motioned for me. The policewoman asked a lot of questions about where I was at the time of the incident and what happened. She was thorough and helpful. She asked a lot more questions and asked if I could identify both suspects for the detective, who was patiently waiting for my answer. He was standing behind her. He was especially interested in the man with the knife.

"He is about my height with my heels on, so five feet four inches. He is about my age, too, close to late forties," I said in a shaky voice, surprised I could remember him. "He is starting to gray and has a weathered face."

"Can you stay with the detective for the evening, in case the suspects are found, so you can positively identify them?" the woman officer asked.

"Sure, I want my car back. And my purse and all my things."

"That's not possible," the detective explained. His large frame barely fit his typical gray suit. "They're on the run and have crashed your car into a pole down on Fillmore Street. It just came over my car phone. The police helicopter will be overhead soon; they spotted the car, they'll likely find them tonight. We should get your purse back for you."

Over the course of the next four hours, I laid in the back of the detective's car in a nearby parking lot so the media overhead did not know I was there. He did not want disruptions in the pursuit. Where were these desperadoes, and how long would this keep gnawing at me like a rabid dog on the hunt? They had violated me and I was angry. They had no respect for me and that was both scary and frustrating.

The detective talked incessantly on his phone for the first hour. Some of it was about my case and some was about other cases of car theft in the area. He sounded like he was piecing together a string of these with the same guy.

I tried to focus my thoughts on what I had to do the next day to get my life back in order. It was not going to be easy, but it settled my pounding heart a bit. Then he started talking to me.

He wanted more details on where I was before I arrived at the store. What was I doing there? Did I come there often? Was I angry enough to want to help to put these people away?

"I teach part-time at Paradise Valley Community College; the semester ended today. I now have a four-week hiatus. I was coming here to relax and talk to the store about working the holidays for a few weeks. I welcome the quiet time away from the busyness of the campus, but I do need something to do. I was looking forward to the sale at the Broadway, too, for some retail therapy. I am still dealing emotionally with trauma from an assault from three years ago."

He acknowledged what I was saying with a glance, but did not respond. I could tell he wanted to focus only on the crime at hand. The chill of the season was in the air as I folded my arms around myself to continue. I was glad I had worn my red wool blazer; it felt good and I was confident, in a way. I had a good job; I was a survivor. Red is power and it fit the Christmas holiday season. I was ready to celebrate a little, but knew this car theft was going to interrupt my life. Crimes against women do that, by taking away our control and coercing us into making decisions we may regret.

I told the detective I had driven down Route 51 from Paradise Valley Community College, as I often did. "After a quick stop at the ATM on Camelback Road, I parked on the west side of the store," I continued. "I was surprised to find a space close to the entrance, since this is a busy shopping center and it is so close to Christmas. But that choice did not protect me. Where was security? Where were Sheriff Joe and his posse? I did not notice the carjackers until they were upon me."

"You could not have done anything more," the male detective said. "This guy had probably tried a car theft a couple times already today and, this time, it just fell into place. We will get this guy. We have had him on our radar."

"The Broadway store is closing for good. They are having a huge sale before Macy's comes in to replace them. This should have been a good night," I babbled, just to talk.

The police search spread out in a four-mile radius around the car. They were overhead and on foot with cars blocking the streets so the media could not intervene. I did not yet know, when the carjackers ran the red light at 24th Street and Camelback, they hit a motorcycle cop who was about to go after them for speeding, and the cop was seriously injured.

Now there was another victim in the case, one of their own. More police were on my car's trail just as the detective came to me at the store. Things moved quickly, like a chess game. I was the pawn, but I played along.

A woman in a van with her young daughter saw the accident. She thought it was a red-light runner and a hit-and-run, so she followed them down 24th Street and identified the car. She called the police from her car phone and then called the ambulance for the officer. She was an angel, with no idea how helpful she was to the case.

"We need you to positively identify them tonight so we can move quickly. They met recently, but he is a repeat offender. She is a runaway. We've been looking for them since last week," the detective explained.

"We want to prosecute and send him back to Florence prison. He's already done time for crimes like this and has only been out of jail six months. We need your help and hope you will cooperate. We'll have an advocate for you all the way," he continued.

I was speechless. How could I be going through all of this crime activity all over again, less than three years after being assaulted? How could the emergency room, the criminal trial and civil trial, the lawyers and doctors and private investigators not flashback and garner attention in my mind again? This was an all-too-familiar situation. How could I be in the middle of more courtrooms and testifying and fear and sleepless nights? I sobbed quietly in the back seat of his car, tears flowing quickly.

"You can use my phone to make a call if that would help," he said.

I called my sister in Michigan and roused her out of bed. She was quiet on the other line as she listened to me tell my tale. She was trying to understand what was happening to me. I could hear it in her deep breathing. She had an uneventful life when it came to crime, but her non-response in no way meant she had no empathy. By her silence, I knew she cared, but it was too painful for her to talk about it. That was her way. Did that matter? Was it me and my lifestyle? A coincidence? Why was crime invading my life again?

The night was filled with small talk as the detective asked me more about my teaching at the college, where I went to school and how I liked living in Old Town Scottsdale. I reciprocated with a few questions, but I didn't say much in response. I knew I was in shock.

He assured me he would get me home safely and that someone with the Phoenix Police Department would be checking on me during the next week. I would be assigned an advocate. I would be safe. But would I feel safe?

"Why didn't anyone see this happen? How could he be so bold?" I asked the detective in frustration. "There were people everywhere."

"These people are pros. They know this is a busy shopping season and that people aren't paying attention. These guys are looking for drug money and they're aggressive. A bad combination! You didn't do anything wrong. You were just the next target; a woman alone, your car door open, your keys and purse handy."

ANSWERS

I was not thoroughly convinced. I knew a few things about violent crime and being a victim. I knew I had played a part by letting my guard down. I had been through a lot with post-traumatic stress on high alert every day since being assaulted. It was my fault in some way, but how?

What did I do to get picked out of the crowd at this exclusive outdoor shopping center? Was it my red blazer? My leaning back in the car to get an item I wanted to return to the store? Or was it the sun shining in my eyes as I came out of the car? My purse plopped down on the trunk? Was it a woman alone? What was it?

The fact that it happens a lot this time of year, about 2,000 times a month in the Phoenix area, did not convince me I was just another statistic. Aren't they supposed to have people there to protect us at the mall? Those people were nowhere to be found. The news media always portrays them on the scene ready to help, but we all know they are often untrained for this scenario.

After another hour or so in the car, the detective received a call. I knew something was finally going to happen, by the gruffness of his voice. He questioned the caller, but started the car. I knew we were leaving the parking lot.

"They've been found hiding in a shed in an alley a couple miles away, but they won't come out," he informed me. "The police will force them out so you can get a good look and identify them for us. We will hold back a bit though, in case there is gunfire. Are you okay back there?"

Although I had already called my sister and knew she cared, I was alone and scared. Remembering her voice helped to calm me as the car started moving toward the street. That would have to be enough for now. I had no idea what would happen. Would I eventually come face-to-face with them in a court of law? This was an enemy of a different kind, a hardened criminal willing to risk going back to prison for what? A chance at more drugs?

The detective was in quick pursuit south down 24th Street to the intersection at Fillmore. A couple miles away he took an abrupt right. We soon passed my mangled car near a darkened light pole. He veered into the dark alley at the end of the street. My mind went back to my car. Would I drive it again? Was my purse in there? Had they taken it with them and later thrown it away? Would I get my possessions back from the car? Do I even want that car back?

Weaving through the alley was a bit tense, but I hung on to the car door handle, getting used to the detective's driving just before he slammed on the brakes. I peered over the front seat, curious and afraid. Squinting into the headlights were two police officers and a disheveled man and woman.

"We're here. There they are. You can sit up, but don't lean forward. We do not want them to see you. Is that them, do you recognize them?"

After a moment of hesitation, I said I did. I said it with fear and trepidation, because I was probably sending the knife guy back to prison and maybe sending the girl to jail for the first time. I was making a huge decision about their lives. I felt queasy about it, as if I were judge and jury, playing God. I felt sick to my stomach. I knew God would guide this investigation. I just had to do my part to the best of my ability and accept God's will for them.

The detective gave me my purse that night. One of the police officers had it with him. I immediately confirmed that nothing was missing. Although I could not take anything from the car that night, I was assured I could go to the car the next day and retrieve my things. It would be in the West Phoenix holding yard. Eventually my insurance company would view it, too, and then it would be scrapped.

The detective was quiet again as we drove to my condo. I was quiet, too, trying to settle down, but I had to ask, "What happens next?"

"You will be assigned an advocate of the court. The state will determine if they have enough evidence to press charges as the plaintiff. They make that decision. They will then contact you about being a witness. The police report and your statement should be enough to go before the judge. You should be prepared to testify in court."

I said nothing more.

DECISIONS

That was a lot to handle for one night. I had already decided I did not want to keep that part-time job at the Broadway store over the holidays. How could I go back there? I was already feeling tense about going home alone. I would buy another used car, and move on with my life.

I would tell my therapist about this so I could sleep better at night. Did I need to go to extensive counseling again? Would this trauma bother me more than I realized? Was I adding to my already high alert state and post-traumatic stress? Time would tell. Like the slow sail that turns deadly, this could be long from over.

The detective got me home safely, walking me to my front door. He shook my hand and placed his left hand on my right arm, telling me I had done a good thing by being a witness. The state could now press charges and do their job. "You will be dealing with the advocate and the court. Try not to dwell on all of that your first night alone."

I thanked him for his efforts. He wished me luck and said that his work was done.

"Good bye."

He left quickly into the dark, cold night.

That was only the beginning. There would be more questions from police, a deposition and questions from attorneys on both sides. Then the trial in Phoenix, the sentencing, the restitution and the waiting for the payments I should receive. There would be years of feeling fear every time I parked my car, or waited for the notice that he had been released from prison. It would not end with the final payment of restitution.

INTERVIEWED

That night, I slept intermittently and kept waking with every sound outside my second story condo. The street was close to the outside gate of the complex and I kept hearing the latch open below my window. When I shut my eyes, the flash of the knife crossed before me. That first night was a restless one.

The next morning the phone rang early. I assumed it was my sister checking on me.

"This is Channel 3 news and we would like to speak to you about the carjacking you were involved in at the Biltmore Fashion Park yesterday." The cheery voice seemed inappropriate. "Are you available to speak with us today?"

"How did you get my number and this information?" I asked. "It was just yesterday."

"We have access to police reports. You're listed in the phone book," she said. "We want just a quick interview. This is an important topic this time of year. Your story could help others."

There it was. Tear at my heart strings, tell me I am the one to help fight violence against women and you got me. Darn you! I am tired. I was taken advantage of yesterday and threatened with a knife. My car is totaled and some somebody rifled through my purse. I want to hide out today.

"Where will we do this? How long will it take?" I asked. "I have a lot to do today with my car and the insurance. Can you come here? I need to rest today, too."

The interview was simple and went pretty well. The news reporter asked a half dozen questions and I answered without preparation. She was professional and did not push me. The cameraman seemed like a gentle soul. I was not shy about the camera. I had been on TV before.

The thing that concerned me most was what would happen that night if the carjackers saw me on TV from their jail cells. Why had I not consulted anyone for advice before doing this interview? Was I so distraught that I could not think straight or make rational decisions?

DEALS

The phone rang again an hour later. It was the lawyer in San Francisco who represented the Westcor Shopping Centers, including the Biltmore Fashion Park. He wanted to hear my story and asked how I was doing. He also asked what expenses I thought I would incur and offered me $3,000 to help me out. He said he had a few papers for me to sign regarding the incident. My mind raced as I listened to him, my gut knotted and a red flag went up.

"I need to think this through before I make any decisions. I want to be sure I am thinking clearly and that I make the best decisions for myself," I said, after giving him the general details he asked for earlier. I did not mention the TV interview.

He persisted, but I did not agree to anything. I felt like I was being abused again by this lawyer. It felt like an attempt by

Westcor to take advantage of me. It was obvious to me that they were interested in their image as a high-end mall. The lawyer had a melodic voice with a sensitive tone, almost a trained voice. But that was not enough to convince me to relinquish my right to ask for more or to sue them for not protecting me on their property.

"I want $6,000, not the $3,000 you offered," I proposed the next day. "I need to replace my car. State Farm is not going to give me what my car is worth. I will need a good down payment to be able to afford another car. I also have a fifty percent split with my Blue Cross insurance on the therapy I need," I told the lawyer in my strongest voice.

"That's a lot of money, and not what we had planned. I need to consult the members of the Board and talk to the mall management in Phoenix. I will get back to you."

I thanked him and hung up. I needed to give this one to God. It was money I could surely use. I did not have any physical injuries, but I needed therapy for the emotional stress and was not sure who would pay for it. I needed another car, too, and I could not afford an attorney. The State of Arizona was the Plaintiff, not me. I was the victim, the chief witness. I would not be represented. Here we go again. God help me.

My friends did not think I should sue. I had been through a civil lawsuit with the previous assault and it was as grueling as the criminal trial. I decided to ask again for twice what they offered me and stand my ground. I waited a few days to call the lawyer back, fretting a lot about the call and the decision. I was really alone. My friends were busy people and my family was far away. They did very little to help me.

My therapist agreed with my decision to ask for more money, when we met for a short session the following week. She encouraged me to stand my ground. "You need to take control and get back some of your life. Take it slow, one step at a time, but be positive. You can do this," she said, with a smile of concern.

She made herself available to me on short notice, so I took advantage of it this time and signed on for an eight-week session to discuss my PTS recovery, my victim feelings that had surfaced again, and what happened that evening at the shopping center. I knew I had taken some steps back in my recovery, but I also knew if I worked through all of this I would eventually be okay from it and learn more about my strengths. I had done it before with the assault, and I knew I could do it again.

The next day the lawyer called and agreed to my price. He had the paperwork already being sent out FedEx. He asked if I would expedite the papers. I called a woman lawyer friend to review them. She did real estate law, but could at least explain the terminology and discuss the verbiage. I took the signed papers back to FedEx the same day. I wasn't looking to fight for money. It was more about jail time for the two people I was about to face in court. The $6,000 would be restitution for my not being protected on Westcor property.

COURT

The court advocate initially met with me at the courthouse in Phoenix to take my deposition, and again when I learned the other victim, the motorcycle cop, had signed his papers. He was going to be okay. He had sustained injuries, but they were healing. He would return to the police department soon, but would not press charges in Civil Court. He did not want to be present for the criminal trial. Unfortunately, I did not have that option. I was the only witness to my assault with a deadly weapon. Carjacking is a layman's term. I had to be there to do my part to secure a conviction.

My third and final time with the advocate was my day in court. The suspects for all crimes presented that day came in shackled together at the ankles, clanging a sad tune. They sat just to my left, about ten feet away.

It was agonizing, as if I was reliving some of that incident all over again. It took a minute before I recognized the weathered little man who had breathed his stale breath on my face and put his shiny knife on my pager. He was clean-shaven now and had a haircut; he looked younger, even boyish in an odd sort of way. The courtroom setting changed my perception of him for just a moment. The man who violated me had that same intense look now as that day at the Biltmore. My chest tightened and I felt an uneasiness in my stomach as if I were about to be disappointed.

The young woman was there in court, too, but seated in a different place and not shackled to a group like her partner in crime. She seemed out of place, attractive with reddish blonde hair. Almost innocent looking, somewhat afraid, too, and stunned by what was going on. Then the letter was read and her lawyer began to weave the tale of how her mother had abandoned her and she ran away. Was she going to get off? Was this girl who riffled through my purse and ran with the wrong guy going to get another chance? Was this supposed to be okay? Was she a victim, too? Did he manipulate her when he found her in the streets? It was not for me to judge.

FINALE

It was over in ten minutes. She was given a suspended sentence, five years of probation, a charge of paying me $3,000 in restitution and $5,000 to State Farm for my car, over a two year period. She was charged with a similar amount for the other victim and his motorcycle. How could she ever pay this? They were sending her back home to New Jersey to be with her mother, a recovering alcoholic who claimed she could now help her daughter and be there for her.

"Why is her freedom a good thing? How will this work? Should I be concerned?"

The advocate seemed unnerved by the judge's decision and my questions.

"You will be fine and she will be monitored to pay. This happens a lot as part of a plea deal, so more prison time and charges go to the main suspect," she said, with no emotion.

The man who pulled the knife on me was returning to the Arizona State Prison in Florence for fifteen years, with a possibility of parole in twelve. If he had slit my clothes or touched my skin with the knife, it would have been twenty-five years. He sat motionless in the line of stoic, shackled men as they read the final decision. I watched that cold, calculating face, unwavering. It was as if he had known his plight before he entered court. It appeared he did not care, as if this was where he knew he would always be. I cringed to think he would someday get out after all those years of thinking about today and come looking for me.

I began to pray for him to forgive himself for all he had done, and to work on his drug problem. Methamphetamine paraphernalia was found in his jacket pocket at the time the police apprehended him in the alley. I prayed for the young girl, too. I hoped that she would recognize the opportunity she now had to make amends to her mother and go down the path to a better life. I prayed that she had learned from her short time on the street. But most importantly, I asked God to help me forgive both of them for scaring me and hurting me, so I could move on.

WISHES DO COME TRUE

In loving, you lean on someone to hold them up.
Rod McKuen

GOD'S PLAN

After two divorces, and more boyfriends then I could count, I was done. I would soon turn fifty. My youngest sister was battling lung cancer back in the upper peninsula of Michigan where we grew up, a long way from Scottsdale, Arizona. My grief was overwhelming.

My life came unraveled. I was losing my best friend and confidante and coming to grips with what life would be like without her. To not have her on the other end of the phone seemed hard to fathom. Before she died she started giving me subtle little bits of advice.

"Stop chasing after those younger guys. They don't make you happy," she whispered one day on the phone, her unique boisterous voice soon to never to be heard again.

"Find yourself an older man who will take you to dinner and a movie. Look for someone who will be nice to you for no reason," she said over and over again.

"There are a lot of older, charming men in Scottsdale in the winter," I chimed in. "But I'm not sure they're for me. My friends don't think so, but my therapist says I'm an old soul."

This was not the first time my sister had alluded to this idea. She had been working on me for years, letting this plan evolve with our many long phone conversations. Ever since she remarried and had her boys, she was quite happy. Then cancer came to call. With little warning, God called her home at forty-four years old. Life changed forever, and the next year, her wish transformed me.

A NEW BEGINNING

A year after her death in 1999, I moved into a newly remodeled condo across from Fashion Square Mall in Old Town Scottsdale. A lot of winter visitors lived there. That worked for me. I had lived for many years in places with young people, but now I looked for peace and quiet. I liked the idea of being in a more adult community.

The condo's owner, a friend in Fargo, North Dakota, offered me a great deal. She carried the loan paper for me to make the financing work. Her husband had died before they could move in, and she could not bear to live there alone. Even though they had just beautifully remodeled the whole place for their winter home, she was ready to sell.

I really liked it; a move up for a new start. The whole plan, a sign from God, happened the way things were to work out.

Within thirty days of learning of its availability, I moved into my new neighborhood and never looked back.

I felt good about how far I had traveled in my healing. My love addiction recovery had less feelings of abandonment. I took my post-traumatic stress condition seriously and nurtured myself to not fall back into fear. I worked diligently on my 12-Step program in Alcoholics Anonymous and enjoyed a full and busy life with a new career teaching marketing classes part-time at the university. I continued to build a consulting business from home.

"I like my life just the way it is. I have no intention of complicating things," I said at lunch with my friends when we celebrated my new place. "I am not looking for Mr. Right; I am not looking for anyone," I continued. "I'm on a spiritual quest and excited about home ownership again."

"Your life has vastly improved. On occasion you must pinch yourself in disbelief," my friend said with a smile. "Your gratitude allows you to receive God's blessings. You sound good. I'm happy for you."

"I miss my sister very much. Her voice keeps whispering to me. I realize everyday how precious time is for me, for all of us," I told my friend, as I showed off my place to her after lunch. "I just don't want to make any more mistakes, waste any more time."

"None of us do, but we eventually have to venture out again. Just be open. That's all you have to do," she continued. "You have shut yourself off for a long time. Maybe it is time to get back in the flow."

I laughed. Nothing was further from my plans for my new neighborhood. I had said hello to the neighbors, but I had not ventured into a conversation with any of them.

NEIGHBORLY

After about six months in my new condo, I noticed a flag flying upstairs in the next building. It was orange and black and said OSU Beavers on it. I knew what that meant, since Notre Dame was coming to town to play Oregon State University in the Fiesta Bowl. Who thought their team could beat my Notre Dame? Unbeknownst to me, a nice snowbird from Oregon was about to enter my life. He lived under the OSU flag and his team was about to win the Fiesta Bowl that weekend. I had no plans to go to the game. I had lost interest in football over the years; post-traumatic stress had seen to that change.

The Oregonian from Unit 310 seemed to be everywhere in the weeks following the flag days. I saw him with his friends heading out to golf. He often worked on the crossword puzzle near the mailboxes by the laundry room, and looked up only to say hello. He always had a nice smile and a slight wave. He usually minded his own business. But one day, on a whim, I asked him to join me and my friends.

"Would you like to go on The Heart Walk with me in Tempe? Several of my friends from the University will be there," I offered. "It's next Saturday at seven a.m."

"I can't. I work that day. I have a part-time job driving a golf cart at the Phoenician Resort," he said with that friendly smile. "Maybe another time; I'm here until the end of April. I live in Oregon and drive back then."

"Yes, maybe," I said. "I just came from teaching a class. I need to run."

I waved and headed for my door. Although not really ready for a conversation, I was glad we had broken the ice. Why did I run away? He seemed okay with a little conversation. Would I have to hear about that darn game? There must be something else we can talk about for a while. He seemed like he had interests, and being from Oregon, a place I had never been, I thought we could talk about his home. I always like to tell people about Michigan and where I grew up. It is so beautiful there.

HEART ATTACK

Over a week went by before I saw Mr. Oregon again. I wondered how things were going for him. I did not suspect anything odd, just thought he was busy with his friends, playing golf and cards.

"How have you been?" I asked, upon seeing him out walking one evening. "Have you been out of town?" I added, hoping he would not think I was being nosy or aggressive.

"Not quite," he smiled. "I had a heart attack. I was in the hospital here in Scottsdale for four days. I'm okay now. Just a little scare."

He must be joking. What are the odds of that happening?

"How odd that I asked you to walk in The Heart Walk last weekend, and instead you had a heart attack."

He was not kidding. "I was taken from the Phoenician by limousine to the emergency room, after lightheadedness and chest pain," he said. "The guys at the valet desk responded quickly. It was a heart attack alright."

"Sounds like you were lucky. It was not your time."

"I didn't need surgery. They did a lot of tests, and a small procedure. I've made some diet changes," he continued, still smiling and amused. "I've made a full recovery. How are you? How was The Heart Walk?" He hurried along to walk beside me.

"I'm good, thank you. The walk last Saturday was fun. About ten of us did it and then went out to lunch in Tempe. It's a good event and raises a lot of money for heart disease," I added, trying not to say too much and appear too chatty.

He seemed interested and was listening; I liked that about him. I didn't move there with the idea that I would meet someone, but maybe some part of a friendship was happening here.

JUST DINNER

The next Friday, I was exhausted after a long week of appointments and teaching classes with a head cold. I went to bed just as soon as I walked in the door. Shortly after I laid my head down, I heard a knock on the door. Damn, who could that be?

195

I peeked down from my upstairs window and there was Mr. Oregon waiting patiently at the stoop. What could he want? I suppose I should answer the door. He must have seen me come home. My parking space is outside his side window.

"Hello, how about dinner with me tonight?" he asked, before I got the door opened all the way. "I need some company. What do you think?"

"I have a heck of a cold and I'm really beat from my busy week," I replied with a reluctant smile.

He did not move or say anything. What was he waiting for?

"Thanks for asking; may I have a rain check?"

"Just dinner. Nothing more," he persisted.

"If we go soon, I suppose a couple of hours would be okay; but I really need some rest."

"Great, I will be back to get you in a half hour. Do you like seafood?"

"Yes, I love it, thanks," I offered with a smile.

He was attempting to cheer me up and it was working.

We walked into the Marco Polo restaurant and were seated immediately. Nice touch. He had made a reservation. It was a popular place, but I had only been there once. Since I did not drink, it was not really my style. It had that singles-bar feel, but more upscale. There was a large bar and dance floor adjacent to the restaurant; but not to worry, we were only having dinner.

"Thanks for coming out with me. I need somebody to talk to tonight," he commented as he held the chair for me. "I just lost my father-in-law."

"I'm sorry to hear that."

"We were good friends; he was a mentor to me for over thirty years." He opened up even further. "I feel a real sadness; depressed, actually, about this loss. He was a great guy."

"I lost my sister less than two years ago, and my mother last year," I added to the conversation. "Grief is a funny thing. A lot of stages and a lot of emotions: hold on for the ride. It takes a while and we all react differently."

"Do you have children?" he inquired, with raised eyebrows.

"No, I don't," I answered. "I was married twice in my twenties, but with no children. Glad it worked out that way. I just had to take care of myself all these years. I have been divorced now for over twenty years. I am okay with all of it."

Does he think me odd, or think nothing of it? He went on to tell me he had three grown children and a granddaughter. He didn't respond to my being childless. He was obviously not judgmental, just curious. We talked through dinner, danced several times, and continued our conversation through dessert. He enjoyed several drinks. I stuck to my usual water and lemon.

"What time is it?" I finally asked, knowing it was way past an early night.

"It's close to ten o'clock. Do we need to leave?" he asked, obviously hoping for a no.

"Yes, it's time to go. I need to get some rest; I've got a busy day tomorrow, too."

By the time we headed to the car, we had talked about everything from marriage and children, to divorce and retirement, even politics and religion. Nothing was off limits and nothing seemed to cause a rift in the conversation.

197

Had my sister sent me this person? Was God putting him in my life for a reason? Surely not for romance; after all he was fifteen years older than me, retired, and still legally married. He was a nice guy, a good person and not like anyone else I had ever been involved with before.

"Thanks for a great night," he said with a hug and little kiss on my cheek. "I hope I can call you soon. I want to do this again," he added.

"Yes, I had a nice time. Call sometime."

WARTS AND ALL

Dinner together became a three times a week invitation and always a night for good conversation. Then it was movies and meeting his friends.

"Golf is his first love," they teased. They had known each other since high school in the 1950s. I was almost a threat.

He met my friends, too, and was well received. He was a gentleman, with a friendly greeting and a big hello. He won them over pretty easily. Somewhere between the first and the tenth dinner I knew I was falling in love with this special person.

This was not the love addiction that had eaten away at me for decades, but a true and authentic respect and caring. We spoke openly about the mistakes we had made in our lives. Everything was on the table when we sat and talked. I was honest with him about my sobriety and what it meant to me. He confessed about his desire to quit drinking. He had wanted to do that for a long time.

He shared with me the story of the deadly car accident he survived in college, that took his best friend and the young woman who had been sitting next to him that day in the car. He, and a woman he hardly knew, had lived. They did not keep in touch.

"It took a long time to realize I could live for them, too," he shared. "It was a difficult recovery. I lost my athletic scholarship and never did go back to OSU. It is a struggle even now to talk about that night. The police never did solve anything. It was a hit and run."

I was intrigued with his story of survival and grief, and encouraged him to talk about it. It became part of our bond and allowed me to share my story of abuse and domestic violence. We were no longer two ships adrift at sea, we were now sailing the same course. We understood post-traumatic stress and we knew grief. Our friendship and trust was now sealed at a deeper level than we could have ever anticipated.

His adventures with his friends in business, his athletic prowess in high school and college, and his true love of the game of golf tumbled out with enthusiasm. He was humble about his accomplishments, but let me know who he was, too. He cared deeply for his children, but did not brag about them. He was proud just the same, and told me about them while he carefully removed pictures from his wallet. His smile radiated a wonderful image of a proud father.

A week later we made plans to go out to the Tournament Players Club for lunch in north Scottsdale. He picked me up with a little smiling bundle in the backseat of the car. His beautiful two-year-old granddaughter became our companion on many outings. His relationship with her endeared me to him. She was lively and whimsical, and added an element of fun to the day. She was a blessing. I hadn't spent any time around children in my adult life.

His children shared reluctance for a while, wondering if a woman fifteen years their dad's junior could be trusted. They took time to accept that their dad was with someone else besides their mother. They had probably anticipated this day, but I doubt it was easy. I did what I could to be a friend. I had no desire to be anyone's mother.

One of his friends didn't like sharing this wonderful man with me. They had quite a life with golf, cards and happy hour. I took up more and more of his time. We socialized with his friends on occasion, and I eventually became friends with them as well. That made a lot of difference.

With my friends, it was more of a concern about his age and what would it be like for me to take care of an older man; how my life would change as the years went on for us.

"Have you thought about what a caregiver does?" my girlfriend asked at lunch. "You have been independent for decades. This is a big change for you. Is this serious?"

"I don't want to project anything into this," I commented. "He's a good friend and companion. I'm not going to walk away from him because of his age. That would be foolish."

My family had the opposite reaction. They were curious about him and happy I had found somebody who treated me well. It didn't matter that he was quite a bit older than me. After all, he was a school teacher like my sister, a golfer like my brother-in-law and someone from the North Country. And from a small town, too. What's not to like?

THE OREGON TRAIL

"Let's see what happens," he usually said. "Okay by me."

We were having a great time during the winter months. I was not under false pretenses. He left each year in late spring.

"If you get tired of the trip, I will put you on a plane and you can fly home," he offered, as we discussed my taking the one-way trip to Portland with him. It was a trip he retraced every spring as a snowbird returning to his home state, 1,500 miles away.

"I'll give it a try. It'll be fun," I said, after a little thought. "How about taking the T-top off of the Camaro for the trip? Let's see how far we can go before we hit rain," I suggested.

"I have never had it off and the car is six years old," he laughed.

"Are you kidding me?" I shrieked. "The drive will be beautiful. We have to go topless."

The trip to Portland took us to Lake Powell the first day and a night at the resort. We stayed through the morning. He was game for a short trip out on a houseboat. The lake was crystal clear and the rock formations were spectacular.

"I usually just drive through," he laughed. "I never do any of this."

On to Salt Lake City and a night there, pulling in late to find only Hooter's near the campus open for dinner service. "Who knew the Tabernacle choir and Hooter's would be in the same neighborhood?" he commented, as we tried to find something to order. It was all part of the adventure.

"Let's stay another half-day tomorrow and tour the Mormon compound," I suggested. "I've never been here." As usual, he was up for another sight-seeing day. Had I met my soul mate?

The Temple doors flew open as we sat relaxing a bit in the sun-drenched square before heading out. A flood of beautiful brides holding hands with elegant bridegrooms followed close behind. Then colorful attendants to meet anxious photographers descended upon the Temple lawn. We were amazed.

"I have never witnessed a mass wedding with the Mormon Church before. It is quite a sight," I gushed. "This is going to be a special memory. Seeing the inside of the Tabernacle was pretty special, too."

"Yes it was, quite the place."

I was so grateful he had agreed to this time with the Latter Day Saints. It was a spiritual time almost, even if we dodged the young women carrying their Bibles.

The T-top stayed off the Camaro for a thousand miles to Boise, Idaho, before we finally hit rain. The conversation flowed continuously; the radio never came on. I realized early in the trip I was going all the way to Portland with him in his green Camaro. I was not going to get tired of driving or of him.

We hit Oregon by early afternoon the last day and made a stop at the beautiful Multnomah Falls. The sun glistened through the clouds and against the tower of rocks that held the falls. They seemed to flow forever.

"I must come back again when I can stay longer," I said sheepishly.

As we headed to the airport for my return flight, I glimpsed Mt. Hood out of the car window. It seemed so close and breathtaking with its snow-capped peak. I was hooked. I felt at home in the place where he had spent all of his life. It was an omen. We were more alike than we realized. We were meant to be together, but a lot of things would have to change before that would happen. The summer separation could clear a lot of thoughts for both of us.

ON THE ROAD AGAIN

The call came at the end of August. It was unexpected; or was it? He had called quite a bit over the summer. We had kept our romance alive by supporting each other long distance. We had continued to laugh together. I knew my sister had picked him for me.

"I am leaving Oregon for good. I want to come live with you," he said in a shaky voice. "I talked to a friend about this. He told me not to let you go. It is what I want to do."

Before I could answer, he added, "I am driving down there in a couple of days. Will you fly up and drive back to Arizona with me? Are you able to make the trip again?"

I had not yet introduced him to my family or taken him to Michigan. I had not thought much about marriage or living with anyone for over twenty years. I was surprised by his call, but I wasn't. I had known when we said goodbye that day in Portland, that we were far from done.

"I quit drinking this summer. I am serious about it," he blurted out in a few minutes. "I want us to have a life together." He kept talking, not waiting for me to answer. "I do not want to lose you."

Was it a proposal? It didn't matter. I could hardly respond in the flurry, but somewhere in it all I said yes.

"When do you want me to help you move? I can fly up there over a weekend."

Our age difference was not an issue for me. His being retired was something we could work around. He wanted to help me with my projects and my work. I wanted to be with him, and could be most of the time, since I had a home-based office. We would make it work, in a way I had never known with any other guy.

"We're hardly ever separated," I told my middle sister after he moved in. "We're having a wonderful time together. You'll like him. I know you will."

October 29, 2005
A Special Memory Wedding Chapel
Las Vegas, Nevada

Epilogue

Think wrongly, if you please,
But in all cases think for yourself.
Doris Lessing

Grief

Grief was with me most of my adult life. During my first marriage, I grieved the death of my best friend. Charm was beheaded in a head-on collision in her VW bug, while driving at night during her teaching at a summer camp. The teenage drunk driver never saw her as he crossed the line. She had inspired me to read more and to pursue my writing. We had just attended a writer's conference in Florida that winter in her VW.

I'd suffered two divorces in my twenties and the loss of my dad in my thirties. A decade later I lost my mother to Alzheimer's disease, and my sister to lung cancer, just one year apart. I knew grief. Life was moving quickly. I had no time to understand it.

The early events set me up for the vulnerability of an abusive relationship. I had not completely healed from one loss before the next one hit. After moving across the country from my family as a young woman, I cut myself off from them emotionally, in order to cope with loneliness. Life was like slow sailing through rough water, a battle against the wind, when all my energy was needed to navigate.

Later, my sadness made it impossible to properly grieve for my sister. By then, I was so emotionally spent from the assault and the trials that I felt helpless at times to even pray for her. It was painful. My mother dying of Alzheimer's disease the year before my sister overwhelmed me, too; I was unable to show any emotion. I was not in touch with how our relationship had gone during my life. She did not know me during most of those trauma years, as she was in the throes her Alzheimer's disease and I was in my isolation. She was not there for me, but I had not expected her to be. We had been distant most of my life.

PAIN

I was inspired again by my friend Charm's husband, who had felt the horrendous pain of grief, but had moved on with his life in a new family. My trauma had turned my life around. It forced me to go through the knothole of grief and to choose helping others to heal and hope.

I took on the challenge of joining other survivors. Those painful experiences catapulted me forward and inspired me to be of service to others. I wrote more. I spoke out for other abused women. I was more honest about who I was and what made me tick.

After the assault, my productivity and socialization were often pushed back into a sea of fear; my shame and guilt exposed. Yet I was inspired by daily affirmations.

I had been brainwashed. It was as if I was watching a vicious storm when I told my stories in therapy. My post-traumatic stress forced me to seek help or die. Therapy became my new normal.

I bought a new condo and moved to a nicer neighborhood. For the first time in six years, I felt light in my step. I was inspired by the other women to speak out about violence against women and learn how to not to hide my feelings. Just as I did with my alcohol recovery, I courageously plowed over the wreckage of my life in love addiction and domestic violence to chart a new course. I wrote about what I knew and I talked about what I felt. My therapist listened.

FORGIVENESS

There was sunshine beyond grief and post-traumatic stress, beyond the darkness of an abusive relationship. I forgave the Enemy and myself to fully experience my life. By being open and vulnerable in therapy and with my group, I lived the forgiveness.

"The Enemy no longer makes me feel like I bring on his anger. I'm inspired to go deeper, to find out who I really am," I told my therapist. "I no longer feel trapped or like I am suffocating in a relationship that once devoured me."

"You'll be okay with him out of your life. He no longer needs to know where you are or what you are doing," she assured me.

I worked to bring forward to my consciousness my story of trauma and violence. I needed to help other women to feel complete. I was inspired by the other survivors I met on my journey. The group therapy sessions showed me how lost I was, how much work I needed to do, and that I could do it. I had restored my hope. I was transformed by what I was learning. I would now carry that message.

"The meetings are led by a woman determined to help us find our souls again," I shared with a friend. "Our therapist gives us questions to ponder and time to reflect before we are encouraged to answer. I am more confident with each meeting. Some of the women are more battered and bruised than I am and some less. We are all trying to find our story to share."

Every time I heard about an act of hostility toward another woman, I became more incensed. Speaking out allowed me to channel my energy and make the anger a positive force by finding forgiveness. I talked about what I was doing with some of my AA recovery women friends, especially the one who had picked me up at the emergency room the night of the assault. It was cathartic.

"The Chrysalis Center sessions are good. I am glad I am there," I commented at lunch. "It was awkward at first, but I know I belong there."

"What do you talk about?" they asked. "Are you embarrassed to tell everything?"

"No, of course not, that is my story. I want to get well and I want to help others."

We had been meeting for lunch for many years. I forgave them for their insensitivity and for any previous criticism. By challenging them to not look away from me, I found some relief. They were not as receptive as I had hoped, but they did listen.

HOPE

Although difficult, I accepted my situation and continued on, hopeful things would improve. God helped me break through. I was being inspired by the other women, who were growing stronger before my eyes.

"I no longer walk on eggshells around anyone. I am not afraid of what I do or say when I do these talks," I told my friends. "The Enemy can no longer fight me, it has long been over. The flowers, phone calls and apologies have stopped, but I have not."

I had been reacting in some enraged manner, either verbally or physically, by acting out what had not yet been fully resolved. I wrote with fierce abandon in my journal for some relief. Writing through episodes of terror moved me closer to God and brought me hope. My writing sustained me, giving me a voice when I felt hopeless.

Writing in my journal for at least three pages helped me. I'd write anything: what was bothering me, what I was grateful for, what I felt good about, what was a source of strength. I heard

God's voice. I wrote openly and honestly. No one else was going to see it.

I exercised daily, rarely missing a day, to take care of my stress levels. This was what I needed to do to survive. Physical exercise gave me more clarity. I sought answers as to why my life was consumed in chaos. I focused on my life.

My meditation in the early morning calmed me. I was lifted and inspired. I could still get a nauseated feeling in the pit of my stomach, like sea sickness, as if there was no end to the turmoil and crushing waves of fear, but I was hopeful. I traversed the chaos by slowly and painfully feeling those emotions in therapy sessions.

I no longer got angry at the wrong target, such as an unassuming person in a retail store. With my eyes on the goal to share what had happened to me, the beacon of light I called hope shone for me. I prayed for the other women in this sea of turmoil, that they, too, would find hope.

SPEAK

I had to speak out. I often spoke professionally. I could do this. I could make a difference, but united we could move mountains. We all needed to do our part and speak up and say "no more."

I no longer accepted sitting by and allowing abuse to be ignored as it had been most of my life. That would be an atrocity.

Domestic violence had to be slowed down. Survivors like me could help by being willing to speak out.

Like wreckage left after a spring storm, the destruction was now at my door. I could not look away. My psyche was a national treasure, a beauty to behold and preserve. The domestic violence issue had to be brought to the forefront of everyone's vision, for peace to come to any of us. It would happen if we joined forces and believed in the miracle; if we were not afraid to tell our stories. Although the statistics on violence and abuse are daunting, I was inspired by the others who spoke out before me.

"After so much abuse, I am no longer afraid of him. I no longer fear for my life," I told my women's group. "I no longer have a restraining order; it was a piece of paper anyway. I am very aware of my surroundings. I take care of myself."

GRATITUDE

My inspiration also came from my faith. It was a part of God's infinite wisdom for me to be grateful for my life each day. My life was meant to be lived in gratitude, not in a state of emotional chaos. I kept a daily gratitude list, and committed to not deviating from a morning ritual of prayer and meditation.

I rose every day at sunrise to have my quiet time. I craved it. My body clock was set to Me Time. I no longer needed the alarm, even though it was set for back-up. My mind and soul were peaceful. I moved on as a survivor in gratitude, thriving a little more each day.

Being grateful influenced my thinking in a positive way. I saw how being of service to others would serve me well. I grew as a person as I thought more about others than myself. This was a critical element to my recovering from trauma.

"The Enemy is good-looking and charismatic; he is gentle with his daughter and kind to his friends. He has a facade and people like him," I told my therapist. "He plays the "perfect guy" for them."

"He no longer has you controlled. You now see what you need to see," she said. "You're going to do great things."

COURAGE

My vision for how to deal with aggressive behaviors became more clear and concise. I was no longer the victim. I was a survivor of violence, thriving as a woman no longer subjected to abuse. I had the courage of my convictions. My personal action steps preserved my dignity and sanity, one step at a time.

His acts of brutality had forced me to deal with my vulnerability. I now realized more chaos was not my destiny. God was carrying me. To come from a basis of courage was the only way to peace for me. I did not falter in these tiny steps. I did not expect perfection, but I was courageous in my efforts.

I no longer buried my story deep in my heart from those who needed to know. With the courage I needed to do God's work for my fellow survivors, I felt confident. I appreciated that telling the truth about the abuse I had endured would heal my heart and cleanse my soul. My truth allowed me to grow, unseen just like the coral reef at the bottom of the sea.

"He no longer plays mind games with me about the vandalism to my car, the other women, the missed phone calls, or his friends' opinions on how they accept his word on everything," I shared in group therapy. "He is not out to get me and manipulate me, he is nowhere to be found. I feel the courage I need to go on."

LOVE

I had to experience the chaos and keep the excitement and the drama real so I could come alive, so I could feel love. I was typical of post-traumatic stress sufferers. It was necessary to purge unpleasant feelings and replace them with virtuous ones.

Tremendous care was required to release my story. Loving me unconditionally was paramount. I would go numb very easily when feeling anything about this part of my life. Giving a reporter's version of the assault, a chronological account of the abuse in the police and court reports was not the whole story. I relived the events from an emotional place to release the negative energy and move to the higher ground of God's grace, God's unrelenting love. I thanked God for the opportunity to be free to love myself. Like the Chicago to Mackinac Sailboat Race, that joy was exhilarating.

"He can no longer make fun of me or manipulate me or tell me I have stupid ideas or am incapable of doing something," I affirmed at one of the last group sessions. "I love myself today."

PASSION

I was passionate about my safety. I put up my security antenna so nothing else would take me by surprise. I now knew the signs to watch for and I was on high alert. This kind of safety valve allowed me to breathe easier and to feel my heart beat at a healthy pace.

Denial was no longer an option for me. I felt passionately that the other parts of grief had to be felt to protect me emotionally, such as the anger in the story. All of the things I had lost had to be dealt with now.

The police report, in staccato like the bleep of the red warning beacon on a light house, was quickly recorded by the police to get the job done. The information condensed into the criminal and civil trials was much the same. The judges made decisions in thirty minutes about the most important thing that had ever happened to me.

I was passionate about telling my story in all its detail, with as much of an accurate accounting as possible. In therapy I had cleared out the secrets to my truth quickly, so they would not be stuck in my soul and haunt me for a long time. My passion for being heard and having a voice was growing stronger.

"I no longer put up with abuse or being degraded. I am a survivor," I told the judge. "He no longer controls me with his threats or intimidation."

The Mayor who helped me died a few years later, with a special place in my heart. He had recognized the necessity of understanding how women are victimized again by the courts. He agreed it was not acceptable to prolong trauma in the justice system. He took his job seriously and was passionate about justice. He helped me when no one else stepped up.

TRUTH

The stories in the police report and the court records are mostly the same. They are partially my truth. Up to this point, I had not been given a chance to tell my entire story. As the victim, I was the main witness. The State of Arizona was the plaintiff. I had no say in the procedures unless asked by the City Attorney. And he didn't ask.

At the end of the criminal trial, I had the right to address the Defendant. In my case, the Enemy represented himself. The criminal trial judge protected me somewhat and made sure I had ample time with my presentation of the impact letter, which I read aloud. My truth was told.

I addressed the Enemy with well-constructed words neatly placed before me on two sheets of a legal pad. Even though I was an accomplished speaker who rarely, if ever, used notes, I was not able to confront him without hesitation. I needed notes that day to be sure I had my say.

The criminal courtroom was not my usual turf and I did not want to forget to say exactly what I had carefully prepared. I felt somewhat vindicated with this opportunity, even though the Enemy had the audacity to ask the judge if he could rebut my statements. This was typical behavior of an abuser's arrogance. As part of the abuser's narcissistic personality, he complained about my victim's rights and denied my truth.

The judge upheld the law and said "No" to this request. It was my right as the victim to address the Defendant in court with no chance of him having the last word. It was one of the few times during this part of my ordeal that I felt some empowerment.

"He no longer makes me feel sorry for him because he has had a tough childhood and feels abandoned. He no longer has the right words to convince me I should take him back one more time," I told my friends after the criminal trial.

I did not anticipate that I would have so much difficulty maneuvering my way through the judicial system. The post-traumatic stress had settled in like a silent killer. My grief for so many losses encouraged the post-traumatic stress growing in me like a cancer, whirling in my psyche just out of reach of help.

I accepted my situation, and let go of my past to reclaim my future. I needed God to know my truth. I did this in church and recovery meetings. I gave myself freely to the sea of change coming my way. I had something more to learn.

My belief was that God does not give us more than we can handle at any time, nor does he give us difficult things until we are ready for them. I accepted that my journey was God's way to try to change something for me from the past, that I was still angry about, something that would not rest in peace. I was open to my truth.

Finding insight into my life and being conscious of what was happening to me was a miracle in itself. I was seeing into my soul, listening to the stillness in my heart. Like a refreshing spray of beach foam on an early morning walk, I now had a chance to hear my own voice.

I was vigilant in my efforts not to recount the story in contradictory and highly emotional ways that eliminated some of the details. I especially worked to tell my part in the story. This was my truth. It had to be brought forward.

It was essential to my recovery that I did not alter my story from the first telling. I asked for God's help and my truth came rushing forth. By being cognizant of the fact that I was a member of a larger band of women, with no guide book to speak of, except notes from the heart, I went deeper. I was inspired by them and saw my part in all of this.

I stood for all the women who could not stand up on their own. I spoke up and shared my story for the women who needed to know they were not alone. The pursuit of my truth has set me free.

Three Husbands and a Thousand Boyfriends

ABOUT THE AUTHOR

Patricia is an award winning author, entrepreneur, business leader, educator and motivator/mentor of women writers.

Patricia created the highly successful Scottsdale Society of Women Writers over ten years ago and continues to serve as its president. She invites professional speakers to the monthly dinner meetings, maintains critique groups and plans outside events for her members. She attends national writing conferences each year and talks locally on writing, publishing and book marketing-related topics. This gives her a wide perspective on the industry.

As founder of Brooks Goldmann Publishing Company, LLC, with her husband, Patricia serves as a publishing consultant. She speaks regularly on writing and publishing-related topics for both aspiring and seasoned writers. Her mission is to enhance the spirit of the author's journey.

Patricia's launch of her second memoir *Three Husbands and a Thousand Boyfriends* magnifies her storytelling of domestic violence and love addiction. She converses regularly with law enforcement, victim's advocates, university students, church communities and other interested parties on a topic she relates passionately to her campaign: *Stop the Violence against Women*.

Her first memoir (now established in second edition print copy and in eBook) is entitled *Gifts of Sisterhood - journey from grief to gratitude*. She is asked often to present with this book on both writing memoir and dealing with grief. Patricia earned a prestigious Arizona Authors Association Literary Contest Non-fiction award for this work.

Current Memberships:

- President/Founder - Scottsdale Society of Women Writers (SSWW)
- Member - Arizona Authors Association
- Member - Phoenix Writers Club (PWC)
- Member - Willamette Writers (WW)
- Member - Arizona Coalition to End Sexual and Domestic Violence (ACESDV)
- Member - Women's Association of Addiction Treatment (WAAT)

Patricia has lived in Arizona for almost forty years, but her heart is still in the Upper Peninsula of Michigan at the Straits of Mackinac where she grew up. She has been happily married to Earl L. Goldmann for the past ten years. They live in Old Town Scottsdale and share their love of reading and foreign films. She is currently writing her third memoir honoring her spiritual journey and alcohol recovery of thirty-plus years.

Recognized Credentials:

- University faculty associate (over fifteen years), Arizona State University, W. P. Carey School of Business and Paradise Valley Community College, Phoenix, Arizona
- Masters Degree in Organizational Management (MAOM)
- The Advanced Toastmasters designation (ATM)
- Named to Who's Who Among America's Teachers

Reach Patricia at patricia@plbrooks.com or 480-250-5556. For for more information, visit:

www.scottsdalesocietyofwomenwriters.com

www.plbrooks.com

www.giftsofsisterhood.com

www.brooksgoldmannpublishing.com

AUTHOR'S REQUEST

PATRICIA L. BROOKS

It is my hope that you will give me feedback now that you have taken this arduous journey with me. Please send comments not only on the book itself, but also on your reaction as a witness to my story of breaking free from a debilitating life.

I do want to hear from you, either personally on email or on a review on Amazon.

Thank you and God bless.
Patricia

www.threehusbandsandathousandboyfriends.com
and/or www.amazon.com
Three Husbands and a Thousand Boyfriends
ISBN 13: 978-0-9817881-8-0
ISBN 10: 0-9817881-8-1

Sexual and
Domestic Violence Services

- **Arizona Coalition to End Sexual and Domestic Violence (ACESDV)**
  www.acesdv.org
  602-279-2900 or 800-782-6400
- **Lay Legal Advocacy**
  Hotline: 602-279-7270
- **National Domestic Violence Hotline-24 hour**
  www.thehotline.org
  800-799-7233 or 800-787-3224
- **National Teen Dating Abuse Hotline-24 hour**
  866-331-9474 or 866-331-8453
- **Rape, Abuse, and Incest National Network Resource Center (RAINN)**
  www.rainn.org
  800-656-HOPE (4673)
- **National Human Trafficking Resource Center**
  www.traffickingresourcecenter.org
  888-373-7888
- **Empowering Youth to End Dating Abuse**
  www.loveisrespect.org
- **T.E.A.R. Teens Experiencing Abusive Relationships**
  www.teensagainstabuse.org

Addiction Resources

- **Sex and Love Addiction Anonymous (SLAA) – Arizona**
  www.slaa-arizona.org
  602-337-7117
- **SLAA Sex and Love Addiction Anonymous (SLAA) – National**
  Fellowship Wide Services: www.slaafws.org
- **National Council on Alcohol and Drug Dependence (NCADD)**
  24-hr./hotline: 800-622-2255
- **Alcoholics Anonymous (AA)**
  www.aa.org
- **Drug Alcohol Hotline**
  www.drugalcoholhotline.com
  855-435-5596

POST-TRAUMATIC STRESS DISORDER RESOURCES

- **American Counseling Association**
  http://www.counseling.org
  800-347-6647

- **American Psychiatric Association**
  http://www.psych.org
  888-357-7924

- **American Psychological Association**
  http://helping.apa.org
  800-374-2721

- **Anxiety Disorders of America**
  http://www.adaa.org
  240-485-1001

- **Freedom from Fear**
  http://www.freedomfromfear.org
  718-351-1717 x20

- **National Center for Victims of Crime (NCVC)**
  http://www.ncvc.org
  202-467-8700

- **National Center for Post-traumatic Stress Disorder (NCPTSD)**
  http://www.ptsd.va.gov
  802-296-5132

Made in the USA
San Bernardino, CA
14 April 2016